# Christmas
## with a
## Country Flavor

BY THE EDITORS OF FARM JOURNAL

edited by Rachel Martens
book design: Alfred Casciato

COUNTRYSIDE PRESS
*a division of Farm Journal, Inc.*
*Philadelphia*

Distributed to the trade by
DOUBLEDAY & COMPANY, INC.
Garden City, New York

# Christmas
## with a
## Country Flavor

# Contents

**Introduction: Christmas with a Country Flavor**          7

**Community Projects**

Light up your yard for the holidays          9
Plan a cooperative Christmas dinner          13
How to run a successful bazaar          133

**Home-Cooked Foods**

**Christmas is sharing**

Cooperative Christmas dinner          13
Sharing family favorites during the holidays          21
Food gifts: Festive breads          26
    Pickled vegetables          29
    Homemade cookies          30
    Two quick and easy candies          31
    Jewel of a gift. . . jellies          32

**Christmas is feasting**

Four heirloom dinners          33
    German trim-the-tree supper          35
    Italian-inspired Christmas week dinner          39
    Swedish-style holiday smorgasbord          42
    Pennsylvania Dutch Christmas feast          47
New turkey dishes          49
Wonderful smell of Christmas baking          52

**Holiday Decorations**

**From Nature's materials**

Let Nature be your holiday decorator          59
Handcrafted Nativity scenes          66
Nature's pottery nests          70

**Handmade decorations**

Ceramics without a kiln          71
Tree trims from fabric scraps          74
Glittering lighted hoops          76
Quilling. . . for lacy Christmas ornaments          78

**Handmade Gifts**

Ceramics without a kiln          71
Quilling. . . gifts          78
Easy to sew gifts for everyone          82
Stitched and stuffed art          88
Old denim. . . one man's junk is another man's treasure          92
New uses for old laces          97
Knitting. . . from a hobby to a business          103
Five things to knit          104
How to make your own "cut glass" candles          116
Make a coiled bread basket          132

**By children**

I made it myself     106

Children's designs have extra appeal     110

**For children**

Make the toys you give     114

# Gift Giving Suggestions

Give a collectible. . . old kitchen utensils     122

Everyone could use another basket     128

# Patterns and instructions

**Rye straw bread basket**     139

**Gifts to sew:**

Hostess apron     143

Hot-pad mitts, landscape apron     144

Patchwork tie     145

Shoe mitts, eyeglass case     147

Placemats, table runner     148

Man's apron     149

Yo-yo pinafore, Christmas tree apron     150

Boy's apron, sports-utility vest     151

Petal skirt for tree     152

Seat pad     153

**Denim gifts:**

Patched shirt-jacket, denim beret     154

Denim dolls     155

Open-top tote, collector's tote     156

Tote with pocket flap     157

**Quilling instructions:**

Fantasy flowers, mini-flakes     158

Plaque, frame     159

Mobile, snowflakes     160

Tree in hoops     163

**Lighted hoops**     164

**Tree trims from fabric scraps**     166

**Knitting:**

Man's pullover     168

Child's pullover     170

Woman's wrap-around sweater     171

Pillow     173

Afghan     174

# Christmas with a country flavor

**A**ll the good things of country living are intensified at Christmas. The warmth of hospitality extends to a widened circle of family and friends. The joy of gifts given and gifts received rests on the thought rather than the cost and brings deep pleasure. There are busy kitchens turning out favorite goodies, and bountiful tables laden for holiday festivity. The house is adorned with decorations family-made from bright bits and pieces as well as from Nature's artistry.

**C**hristmas country-style means, above all, sharing. It may be a gift from the kitchen—cookies, a favorite relish, homemade candy or holiday breads. Perhaps a simple gift lovingly stitched for someone's use and enjoyment. The season abounds with donations of time and personal skills for a bazaar to benefit children, the aged or the church. The universal theme is sharing and caring and we've collected hundreds of friendly and neighborly ways to do it country-style.

**C**hristmas is for feasting with family and friends gathered around the table. We give you tried and tested recipes guaranteed to brighten the eyes of all who gather at yours. If you'd like to revive traditions and experience the taste pleasures your ancestors knew, you'll enjoy trying the adapted ethnic holiday menus offered here—German, Swedish, Italian, Pennsylvania Dutch. Also, in these times when the rush and busy-ness of everyday living lessens our opportunities to better know and enjoy our friends, you might find the cooperative Christmas dinner a welcome and happy event. You'll find inspiration aplenty in the menu offered—all that remains is to organize your group.

**T**o search for a word to describe the country flavor of Christmas is to find many—friendliness, love, neighborliness and, perhaps most of all, involvement. Simplicity, too, is a keynote of the ideas offered here. There are crafts for people with talented fingers and for people whose talents are as yet undiscovered. Your tree can be resplendent with trims you've made from throwaway materials; your house can testify to the majesty of Nature even in winter. And to show you how spectacular sharing can be, we recount the neighborly cooperation in a small Kansas town, that has grown into an annual outdoor decoration festival. Duplicate it in your town or neighborhood—all it takes is imagination and the spirit of sharing.

**T**his book has been created from the celebrative experiences of real people—country families who, because they are farther from the madding crowd, make a little more of Christmas in the "old-fashioned" way. For Christmas is the time to express honest sentiment, love and joy.

# Light up your yard for the holidays

**Y**ou'll discover a new twist to outdoor decorating with lights in the rural town of Russell, Kansas. Drive through the residential area, and find Starlight Trees (pictured above). . . then on to Candy Cane Lane, Tin Can Alley, Little Sugar Plum Lane, and even Rudolph Avenue. Streets are temporarily renamed during the holidays, some with new signs.

The effects created are almost breath-taking, but the actual decorations are quite simple—and

Candy Cane Lane is pictured at night (right). The closeup (below) shows each cane is made of stovepipe, with holes drilled for lights. Alternating red and green bulbs create the stripes.

Holly Wreath Lane has long rows of huge wreaths, all made from old tires. These are painted red or green, then wrapped with greens, tinsel and lights. They're supported with lengths of pipe. The next photo is on Drummer Boy Lane, where tall plywood cutouts march in a toy parade.

Tin Can Alley (below) looks glamorous at night. The detail at left shows individual tin can lids attached to lengths of lightweight chains (available at hardware stores). Chains run from the top of a center pole to ground stakes (or a weighted circular base). You can brighten lids with glitter.

Photography/Chester Peterson Jr.    Data/Nancy Peterson

borrowable for any town, or individual family. Impact, however, comes from repetition. Every home owner in a block (or several blocks) makes the same decoration for his front yard. Rather than compete with each other for the biggest and best single display, neighbors work together as teams to produce streets of themed harmony.

It all began when Main Street got new holiday trimmings a few years ago. Residents decided it would be fun to spread Christmas lights all over town. Decoration themes have come from old Christmas cards, magazines, and even available junk. Wreaths, for instance, are fashioned from old tires, some of which have been rescued from

trash piles. Investment may be as little as $1. Highest-priced items to make are the plywood cut-outs—these run up to $35 for materials.

Often, a sign bearing the home owner's name is worked into the design. And lights are important to all displays. Sometimes strings of tree lights become part of the design; other displays stand in floodlights. "When the idea caught on, you couldn't buy an extension cord for 40 miles," says Bob Krug, wheat farmer who lives in town.

These displays, lighted the first Sunday in December, delight residents and visitors until New Year's. About two-thirds of Russell's 2300 homes have a display in this community-wide project.

Plywood cutouts on one street (above)
take the form of golden angels complete with
trumpets and tinsel. At left, plywood
"snowmen" represent the family members
and pets in each household. Little Amy
Musselman arranges some Christmas greens
on this plywood family group.

# Plan a cooperative Christmas dinner

Do you remember when Christmas was a huge family affair? Everyone gathered at one home for the big Christmas feast. Aunts, uncles, cousins—the whole clan was there, and everyone brought their "famed" recipes. Christmas just wouldn't be Christmas without Aunt Bessie's rich pecan pie, Cousin Emma's candied sweet potatoes (she never *would* part with the recipe!) and Clara's coleslaw with her famous homemade dressing. Tables were filled with good things to eat; the rooms were jangling with the sound of happy chatter as everyone caught up on the family news.

Hopefully your Christmas is still a time for sharing. . . good food. . . good friends. . . good conversation and thoughtful gift exchanges. What better way to combine them all on Christmas Day than to invite a number of relatives and friends to share their most treasured holiday recipes. If each family or guest brings a very special dish, you can all enjoy a bountiful holiday meal together.

Or, as hostess you may wish to plan the dinner menu yourself and send handmade invitations with a recipe enclosed for each family or guest to make and bring to your house on Christmas day.

We've planned a Cooperative Christmas Dinner Menu you might like to follow. . . a scrumptious buffet meal with all the "trimmings." We selected ham that's stuffed with a delicious gently-herbed dressing—it looks elegant. You could bake the ham and let guests bring the rest of the meal.

The decorations and table setting create the mood for a festive dinner but needn't be fancy. With lots of greens and simple ribbons, plus imagination, your home and table can look spectacular. We made gingerbread men and placed them midst the greens for a different decoration.

As the centerpiece for your Christmas buffet, why not buy an inexpensive basket as we did and spray paint it to coordinate with your color scheme. Fill the basket with a small remembrance for each guest. We decided to give the men crunchy homemade peanut brittle, tied up in a red bandanna—actually two gifts in one! Each youngster can pick a gingerbread man from the centerpiece and women guests will receive all the holiday dinner recipes, tied up with a bright red ribbon.

# Christmas is sharing

An old fashioned way to enjoy Christmas day—
everyone shares in fixing the food. Basket holds
take home favors: menu recipes for the women,
bandana-wrapped peanut brittle for the men,
gingerbread men for the children.

# MENU

*Zippy Tomato-Lemon Cocktail**
*Glazed Stuffed Ham**
*Candied Yams with Pecans**
*Fruited Cabbage Salad**
*Molded Artichoke and Bean Salad**
*Tangy Cranberry Conserve**
*Cream Puffs with Tutti-Frutti Filling**
*Cranberry-Raspberry Pie**

*See recipes

Photography/Richard Tomlinson  Photo Stylist/Sylvia Stern

## Zippy Tomato-Lemon Cocktail

*Make this ahead and keep it chilled*

| | |
|---|---|
| 1 (46 oz.) can tomato juice | 1½ tblsp. Worcester-shire sauce |
| 2 tblsp. lemon juice | Thin lemon slices |
| 1 tsp. grated lemon rind | |

• Combine all ingredients in large pitcher. Cover with plastic wrap. Chill at least 2 hours in refrigerator. Makes 8 to 12 servings.

## Glazed Stuffed Ham

*A tasty dish which requires little of the hostess's time*

| | |
|---|---|
| 1 (12 lb.) fully cooked bone-in ham | ½ tsp. dried thyme leaves |
| ½ c. chopped onion | ¼ tsp. salt |
| ½ c. chopped celery | 1 egg, beaten |
| 2 tblsp. chopped fresh parsley | ¾ c. milk |
| ½ c. butter or regular margarine | 1 c. brown sugar, firmly packed |
| 6 c. soft bread cubes (¼″) | ½ c. dark corn syrup |
| 1 tsp. rubbed sage | ½ c. orange juice |
| | Watercress or parsley |

• Place ham fat side up on rack in roasting pan. Bake in 325° oven 2 hours 30 minutes or until meat thermometer reads 120°.
• Saute onion, celery and parsley in melted butter until tender (do not brown).
• Combine sauteed vegetables, bread cubes, sage, thyme, salt, egg and milk. Toss until well mixed.
• Combine brown sugar, corn syrup and orange juice in saucepan. Heat until sugar melts.
• Make 1½″ deep diagonal cuts in ham about 1½″ apart. Press stuffing into cuts. Brush ham with glaze.
• Bake in 325° oven 40 minutes or until meat thermometer reads 130°, brushing ham frequently with glaze.
• Place ham on platter. Garnish with watercress. Makes 12 servings, plus enough for leftovers.

15

## Candied Yams with Pecans

*Prepare day before and cover; easy to carry*

| | |
|---|---|
| 5 lbs. yams or sweet potatoes (10 medium) | ½ c. hot water |
| 1 tsp. salt | 2 tsp. grated orange rind |
| 1 lemon, sliced | ¼ tsp. ground cinnamon |
| Whole cloves | 1 c. coarsely chopped pecans |
| 2 c. brown sugar, firmly packed | 2 tblsp. butter or regular margarine |
| 1 c. dark corn syrup | |

• Place yams and salt in Dutch oven with water to cover. Bring to a boil. Reduce heat; cover and simmer 30 minutes or until yams are tender. Drain and cool.

• Remove peels. Cut in ¼″ slices. Place yam slices in rows in greased 13×9×2″ baking dish. Cut lemon slices in half and stud with cloves. Place 2 or 3 lemon slices in each row.

• Combine brown sugar, corn syrup, water, orange rind and cinnamon in saucepan. Cook over medium heat until sugar is dissolved, stirring occasionally. Cool slightly.

• Sprinkle pecans over yams. Then pour syrup over all. Dot with butter. Cover with foil; refrigerate several hours or overnight.

• Remove foil. Bake in 400° oven 30 minutes or until hot and bubbly. Makes 8 to 12 servings.

## Fruited Cabbage Salad

*Carry to the party and toss at the last minute*

| | |
|---|---|
| 12 c. shredded cabbage | ½ tsp. salt |
| 2 oranges, peeled and cut in segments | ½ tsp. dry mustard |
| ½ c. sliced celery | ⅛ tsp. pepper |
| 2 tblsp. minced fresh parsley | 2 c. apple juice |
| ⅓ c. sugar | ⅔ c. white vinegar |
| 2 tblsp. cornstarch | 2 eggs, beaten |
| | 2 red apples, cored and cut in wedges |

• Combine cabbage, oranges, celery and parsley in large bowl. Cover; chill in refrigerator several hours.

• Combine sugar, cornstarch, salt, mustard and pepper in saucepan. Stir in apple juice and vinegar. Beat in eggs with rotary beater. Cook over medium heat, stirring constantly, until mixture coats a spoon. Remove from heat. Cool.

• Pour dressing into jar. Cover and chill in refrigerator.

**To serve:** Add apples and dressing to cabbage mixture; toss gently to mix. Serve immediately. Makes 8 to 12 servings.

## Molded Artichoke and Bean Salad

*Carry this to cooperative dinner in its mold*

| | |
|---|---|
| 3 (3 oz.) pkgs. lemon flavor gelatin | 2 hard-cooked eggs |
| 4½ c. boiling water | 8 pimiento strips |
| ¼ c. white vinegar | 1 (8½ oz.) can artichoke hearts, drained and quartered |
| 2 tblsp. lemon juice | |
| ¼ tsp. salt | 1 (8 oz.) can cut green beans, drained |
| 2 tblsp. minced onion | |

• Dissolve gelatin in boiling water in bowl. Stir in vinegar, lemon juice, salt and onion. Remove 2 c.; chill until syrupy. (Leave remaining gelatin mixture at room temperature.)

• Slice eggs; reserve 8 slices. Chop remaining eggs; set aside.

• Pour half of syrupy gelatin in lightly oiled 2-qt. ring mold. Alternately place 8 egg slices and pimiento strips in gelatin. Pour rest of syrupy gelatin on top. Refrigerate.

• Chill remaining gelatin until syrupy. Fold in artichokes, green beans and chopped eggs. Pour into mold. Chill until set. Makes 8 to 12 servings.

## Tangy Cranberry Conserve

*This relish combines two traditional holiday foods*

| | |
|---|---|
| 2 c. fresh or frozen cranberries | 2 c. prepared mincemeat |
| ½ c. sugar | 1 tsp. grated orange rind |

• Combine all ingredients in saucepan. Bring mixture to a boil. Reduce heat and simmer 10 minutes or until cranberries are tender, stirring occasionally. Cool slightly. Store in refrigerator. Makes 8 to 12 servings.

Red and white is the theme for this warm Christmas look. Shiny red apples form the base for white candles, trimmed with saucy red bows of red and white gingham. Red bandana napkins add a bright note to the solid red tablecloth.

## Cream Puffs with Tutti-Frutti Filling

*Assemble and keep refrigerated until served*

½ c. butter or regular
  margarine
1 c. boiling water
½ tsp. salt
1 c. sifted flour
4 eggs
1 (3¼ oz.) pkg. vanilla
  pudding and pie
  filling
1½ c. milk
1 (11 oz.) can mandarin
  orange sections,
  drained and halved

½ c. currants
¼ c. chopped candied
  pineapple
¼ c. chopped green
  candied cherries
1½ tsp. rum flavoring
1 c. heavy cream,
  whipped
Thin Vanilla Icing
  (recipe follows)
4 red candied cherries,
  halved
1 green candied cherry

• Heat butter with boiling water in 2-qt. saucepan, stirring occasionally, until butter melts. Reduce heat to low. Add salt and flour all at once. Stir vigorously until mixture leaves sides of pan in a smooth ball.

• Remove from heat. Add eggs, one at a time, beating with electric mixer until smooth after each addition. After all the eggs have been added, beat until mixture has a satinlike sheen. (If you wish, you can beat with a spoon or whisk.)

• Drop mixture by tablespoonfuls, 3″ apart, on greased baking sheet.

• Bake in 400° oven 50 minutes or until golden brown and puffy. (Do not open oven during baking.) Remove from baking sheets; cool on racks.

• Prepare vanilla pudding and pie filling with 1½ c. milk according to package directions. Cool well.

• Fold mandarin oranges, currants, pineapple, ¼ c. green candied cherries and rum flavoring into cooled pudding. Then fold in whipped cream.

• Cut cooled cream puffs in half. Spoon filling into bottom half. Top with other half.

• Spoon Thin Vanilla Icing over top of each. Place halved red candied cherry on top. Cut green candied cherry into leaves and place one next to each red cherry. Refrigerate. Makes 8 servings.

**Thin Vanilla Icing:** Combine 1 c. sifted confectioners sugar, 1½ tblsp. milk and ½ tsp. vanilla; beat until smooth.

## Cranberry-Raspberry Pie

*Absolutely scrumptious—take in a pie carrier or box*

2 c. fresh or frozen
  cranberries
1 (10 oz.) pkg. frozen red
  raspberries, thawed
1½ c. sugar
2 tblsp. quick-cooking
  tapioca

¼ tsp. salt
¼ tsp. almond extract
Almond Pastry (recipe
  follows)
1 tblsp. butter or regular
  margarine

• Chop or coarsely grind cranberries. Combine cranberries, raspberries, sugar, tapioca, salt and almond extract; mix well.

• Prepare Almond Pastry.

• Spoon filling into pastry-lined pie plate. Dot with butter. Roll out remaining dough, cut in ½″ strips. Interlace strips in crisscross fashion over filling to make lattice top. Trim strips even with pie edge. Turn bottom crust up over ends of strips. Press to seal edges. Flute edge.

• Bake in 425° oven 10 minutes. Reduce heat to 350° and bake 40 minutes or until golden brown and filling is bubbly. Makes 8 servings.

**Almond Pastry:** Sift together 2¼ c. sifted flour, 1 tsp. salt and 1 tblsp. sugar. Cut in ¾ c. shortening until mixture resembles fine crumbs. Beat together 1 egg yolk, 2 tsp. almond extract and ¼ c. water; sprinkle over flour mixture. Toss with fork to make a soft dough. Divide dough in half; form each half into a ball. Roll to about ⅛″ thickness on lightly floured surface and line 9″ pie plate.

These two dramatic desserts are a welcome
change from the traditional mince and pumpkin
pies. Cream Puffs with Tutti-Frutti Filling are light
as air; the subtle flavor of the raspberries is the
perfect complement to the tangy cranberries in
the Cranberry-Raspberry Pie.

Photography/William Hazzard

# Sharing family favorites during the holidays

Late autumn is the time when country kitchens hum with preparation for the two big feasting seasons of the year, Thanksgiving and Christmas. Precious heirloom recipes are pulled from files . . . delightful smells drift through the house . . . Dad's cracking nuts for the treasured fruitcakes . . . the youngsters are shaping popcorn balls . . . Mother is deciding whether to use Grandmother's sage or chestnut dressing for the turkey. Everyone's excited about the forthcoming holidays.

It's a time for family get-togethers over memorable meals. We present a collection of family recipes that through the years— sometimes over generations— have been lovingly prepared and shared with friends, relatives and guests. We have included a holiday menu complete with recipes.

A very special holiday dinner. Clockwise: Roast Turkey, Spicy Orange Mold, Broccoli and Onion Surprise, Cheese and Potato Scallop and Hot Yeast Rolls.

21

## MENU

*Roast Turkey*
*Cheese Potato Scallop\**
*Broccoli and Onion Surprise\**
*Spicy Orange Mold\**
*Cranberry Chutney\**
*Hot Dinner Rolls\**
*Golden Ice Cream Squares\**

°See recipes

## Cheese Potato Scallop

*Garnish with parsley and thin pimiento strips*

| | |
|---|---|
| 15 medium potatoes, pared and sliced (about 5 lbs.) | 2 tsp. dry mustard |
| | 6 c. milk |
| ½ c. butter or regular margarine | 1 lb. Cheddar cheese, shredded (4 c.) |
| 1½ c. chopped onion | 1 c. saltine cracker crumbs |
| ½ c. flour | ¼ c. melted butter or regular margarine |
| 2½ tsp. salt | Paprika |
| 2 tsp. Worcestershire sauce | |

• Cook potatoes in boiling water until tender. Drain well.
• Melt ½ c. butter. Add onion; saute until tender. Blend in flour, salt, Worcestershire sauce and dry mustard. Gradually stir in milk. Cook, stirring constantly, until sauce thickens and boil 1 minute. Remove from heat. Add cheese; stir until melted.
• Place potatoes in two 11×7×1½″ baking dishes. Pour on cheese sauce. Sprinkle with crumbs combined with ¼ c. butter; top with paprika.
• Bake in 350° oven 30 minutes or until golden. Makes 12 servings.

**Note:** If you wish, freeze one unbaked casserole for later use. To serve: Bake in 350° oven 45 minutes or until hot and bubbly.

## Broccoli and Onion Surprise

*Bright green broccoli is always a holiday favorite*

| | |
|---|---|
| 3 (10 oz.) pkgs. frozen broccoli spears or 4 lbs. fresh broccoli | ½ c. melted butter or regular margarine |
| 2 (1 lb.) cans whole onions | ¼ c. lemon juice |

• Cook frozen broccoli according to package directions. If you use fresh broccoli, wash it well. Trim off tough stalks. Slit thick stalks with knife. Cook, uncovered, in large saucepan in boiling salted water for 5 minutes. Cover and continue cooking for 8 minutes or until tender. Drain well.
• Meanwhile, heat onions in saucepan. Drain. Arrange broccoli and onions on serving platter. Combine butter and lemon juice. Pour over all. Makes 10 to 12 servings.

## Spicy Orange Mold

*This salad is a natural with crusty baked ham*

| | |
|---|---|
| 1 (1 lb. 13 oz.) can sliced cling peaches | 3 cinnamon sticks |
| ¼ c. vinegar | 4 (3 oz.) pkgs. orange flavor gelatin |
| ½ c. sugar | ¼ c. chopped pecans |
| 12 whole cloves | |

• Drain peaches, reserving juice. Cut peaches into chunks; set aside.
• Combine juice, vinegar, sugar, cloves and cinnamon sticks in saucepan. Bring to a boil; reduce heat. Simmer 10 minutes. Strain syrup. Add enough boiling water to make 3½ cups. Dissolve gelatin in hot syrup. Stir in 2 c. cold water. Chill until thick and syrupy.
• Fold in peaches and pecans. Turn into 6-cup mold. Chill until set. Makes 10 to 12 servings.

## Golden Ice Cream Squares

*During the holidays, top with a bright red cherry*

| | |
|---|---|
| 1 c. vanilla wafer crumbs | 1 tsp. almond extract |
| ⅓ c. toasted slivered almonds | 1 qt. vanilla ice cream, softened |
| 3 tblsp. melted butter or regular margarine | 1 (12 oz.) jar apricot preserves |

• Combine crumbs, almonds, butter and almond extract. Mix well. Reserve ¼ c. crumb mixture. Sprinkle half of remaining crumbs in bottom of 8″ square baking dish. Spread half of ice cream over crumbs, using a wet spatula. Drizzle with half of preserves. Repeat layers. Top with reserved ¼ c. crumb mixture. Cover with aluminum foil. Store in freezer.

**To serve:** Cut in squares. Top with whipped cream, if you wish. Makes 9 servings.

## Potato Filling

*Traditionally served instead of bread stuffing*

2 eggs
10 c. seasoned mashed potatoes
3 c. chopped onion
3 c. chopped celery
⅔ c. butter
6 c. soft bread cubes (½″)
½ c. minced fresh parsley
2 tsp. rubbed sage
½ tsp. salt
¼ tsp. pepper
2 tblsp. butter
2 tblsp. milk
Paprika

• Mix eggs with mashed potatoes; set aside.
• Saute onion and celery in ⅔ c. butter. Add next 5 ingredients; toss until golden.
• Combine with mashed potato mixture. Turn into a buttered 3-qt. casserole. Dot with 2 tblsp. butter and sprinkle with milk and paprika. Bake in 375° oven 40 minutes or until golden. Makes 10 servings.

## Mushroom Bread Stuffing

*This unusual dressing has been a family favorite*

1 c. chopped onion
1 (4 oz.) can sliced mushrooms, drained
½ c. melted butter
12 c. soft bread cubes
¼ c. minced fresh parsley
1 tsp. rubbed sage
¼ tsp. pepper
1 (10½ oz.) can condensed cream of mushroom soup
1 tblsp. milk

• Saute onion and mushrooms in ¼ c. melted butter. Toss together bread cubes, parsley, sage, pepper, ¼ c. butter and sauteed vegetables. Stir soup and add to mixture.
• Place in a greased 2-qt. casserole and sprinkle with milk. Bake in 350° oven 35 minutes or until brown. Makes 6 to 8 servings.

## Ruby Cranberry Crunch Salad

*This can also be made in individual molds*

2 (3 oz.) pkgs. cherry flavor gelatin
2 c. boiling water
1 c. cold water
2 tblsp. lemon juice
1 (1 lb.) can whole cranberry sauce
1 c. finely diced celery
½ c. chopped walnuts

• Dissolve gelatin in boiling water. Stir in cold water and lemon juice. Chill until thick and syrupy.
• Fold cranberry sauce, celery and walnuts into gelatin mixture. Pour into a lightly oiled 2-qt. mold. Chill until set. Makes 8 to 10 servings.

**To serve:** Unmold gelatin on plate. Garnish with celery leaves and sugared raw cranberries.

## Creamy Apple Salad

*An old-fashioned salad that is sure to please all*

1 (13½ oz.) can pineapple tidbits
6 unpared red apples, cut in wedges (5 c.)
1 c. chopped walnuts
1 c. chopped celery
½ c. quartered maraschino cherries
¾ c. mayonnaise
2 tblsp. lemon juice
½ tsp. salt
½ tsp. grated onion
1 c. frozen whipped topping, thawed

• Drain pineapple, reserving ¼ c. juice. Combine pineapple, apples, walnuts, celery and maraschino cherries in a large bowl.
• Combine mayonnaise, lemon juice, salt, onion and reserved pineapple juice; blend well. Fold in whipped topping. Pour dressing over apple mixture; toss gently. Serve on lettuce leaves. Makes 8 to 10 servings.

## Nutty Yam Bake

*This dish can be made ahead and refrigerated*

3 large sweet potatoes or yams
1 c. sugar
¼ c. butter or regular margarine
1 tsp. ground cinnamon
½ tsp. ground allspice
¼ tsp. ground nutmeg
2 c. milk
2 eggs
½ c. flour
½ c. sugar
¼ c. butter or regular margarine
½ c. chopped walnuts
½ tsp. ground cinnamon
Butter or regular margarine

• Cook sweet potatoes in boiling water until tender. Drain well.
• Mash sweet potatoes while hot. Add 1 c. sugar, ¼ c. butter, 1 tsp. cinnamon, allspice and nutmeg; mix well. Beat in milk and eggs; whip well with mixer. Turn into greased 3-qt. casserole.
• Combine flour, ½ c. sugar and ¼ c. butter until crumbly. Mix in walnuts and ½ tsp. cinnamon. Sprinkle over top of sweet potato mixture. Dot with butter.
• Bake in 375° oven 35 to 40 minutes. Makes 6 servings.

## Creamy Carrots and Onions

*Garnish with parsley and chopped pimientos*

1 lb. carrots, cut in strips
2 c. sliced onion
2 tblsp. butter
⅛ tsp. pepper
1 (10½ oz.) can condensed cream of chicken soup

• Cook carrots and onions in boiling salted water in saucepan for 10 minutes or until tender. Drain and reserve ⅓ c. cooking water. Combine reserved cooking water, butter, pepper and soup with cooked vegetables. Heat well, stirring occasionally. Makes 6 servings.

## Christmas Cabbage Salad

*Adds a colorful note to the holiday table*

| | |
|---|---|
| ½ c. sugar | 2 eggs, beaten |
| 1 tblsp. flour | 6 c. shredded cabbage |
| 1 tblsp. cornstarch | 1 c. miniature marsh- |
| ½ tsp. salt | mallows |
| ⅛ tsp. pepper | 1 unpared red apple, |
| ⅛ tsp. dry mustard | cored and cut in |
| 1 (8½ oz.) can pine- | wedges |
| apple tidbits | Pecan halves |
| ¾ c. white vinegar | |

• Combine sugar, flour, cornstarch, salt, pepper and mustard in a saucepan. Drain pineapple; add enough water to make 1½ c. juice. Stir juice and vinegar into dry ingredients. Beat in eggs. Cook over medium heat, stirring constantly, until mixture thickens. Cool well.
• Toss with cabbage, marshmallows, apple and pineapple. Garnish with pecans. Serve immediately. Makes about 8 servings.

**Serving Idea:** Halve 4 large oranges; remove pulp, leaving good firm shells. Remove all membranes. Fill orange shells with salad. Garnish each with reserved chopped orange sections and a sprig of parsley or watercress.

## Hot Dinner Rolls

*Shiny topped yeast rolls with a feathery texture*

| | |
|---|---|
| 1 pkg. active dry yeast | 3 eggs |
| 1 c. lukewarm water | 1 c. sugar |
| 1 tblsp. salt | 1 c. cooking oil |
| 1 tblsp. sugar | Melted butter or regular |
| 3 c. water | margarine |
| 14 c. sifted flour | |

• Sprinkle yeast on 1 c. lukewarm water; stir to dissolve. Stir in salt, 1 tblsp. sugar, 3 c. water and 4 c. flour. Beat thoroughly (mixture should be bubbly). Cover and let stand in warm place 3 hours.
• Beat eggs, 1 c. sugar and oil into batter, blending well. Gradually add enough remaining flour to make a soft dough that leaves the sides of the bowl. Turn dough onto lightly floured surface and knead until smooth and satiny, about 8 to 10 minutes.
• Divide dough into sixths. Cut each into 36 parts and shape into balls. Place 3 balls in each greased 3″ muffin-pan cup. Let rise until doubled.
• Bake in 375° oven 18 minutes or until golden. Brush tops with melted butter. Makes 6 dozen.

## Cranberry Chutney

*Perfect accompaniment for a roast turkey dinner*

| | |
|---|---|
| 1 (1 lb. 14 oz.) can fruit | ¼ tsp. cayenne papper |
| cocktail | 2 c. raw cranberries |
| ½ c. orange juice | 1 c. chopped, unpared |
| ½ c. sugar | apples |
| ¼ c. light brown sugar, | 1 tblsp. finely chopped |
| firmly packed | candied ginger |
| ¼ c. cider vinegar | 1 small clove garlic, |
| ½ tsp. ground cloves | minced |
| ½ tsp. salt | ¾ c. raisins |

• Drain fruit cocktail, reserving 1¼ c. syrup. Combine reserved syrup, orange juice, sugar, brown sugar, vinegar, cloves, salt and cayenne pepper in 3-qt. saucepan. Bring to a full boil, stirring often.
• Add cranberries, apples, ginger, garlic and raisins. Cook until cranberries pop, about 5 minutes. Stir in fruit cocktail. Simmer, stirring often, until mixture thickens slightly, about 15 minutes.
• Pour into hot, sterilized jars. Seal immediately. Store in refrigerator. Chutney will thicken as it cools. Makes about 5 cups.

# Sharing thoughtful
# Gifts of food

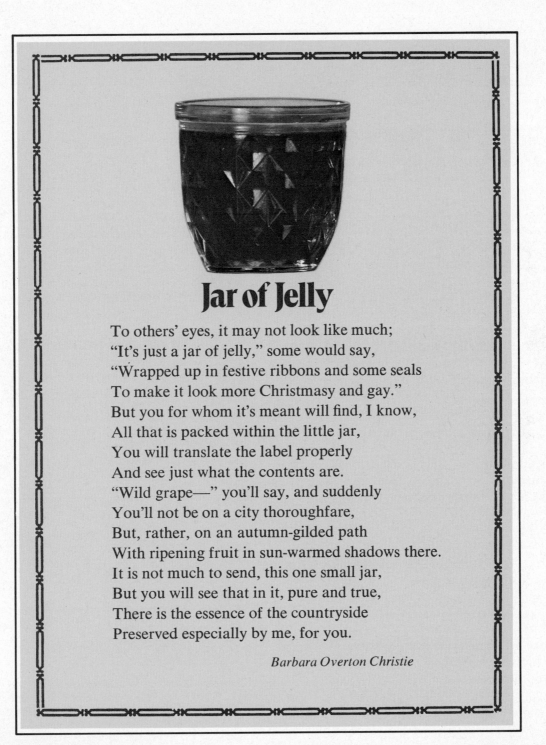

## Jar of Jelly

To others' eyes, it may not look like much;
"It's just a jar of jelly," some would say,
"Wrapped up in festive ribbons and some seals
To make it look more Christmasy and gay."
But you for whom it's meant will find, I know,
All that is packed within the little jar,
You will translate the label properly
And see just what the contents are.
"Wild grape—" you'll say, and suddenly
You'll not be on a city thoroughfare,
But, rather, on an autumn-gilded path
With ripening fruit in sun-warmed shadows there.
It is not much to send, this one small jar,
But you will see that in it, pure and true,
There is the essence of the countryside
Preserved especially by me, for you.

*Barbara Overton Christie*

# Give festive breads

## Pineapple Date Loaf

*A pretty bread that tastes like a mellow fruitcake*

| | |
|---|---|
| ¼ c. soft butter | 2½ tsp. baking powder |
| ½ c. sugar | ¼ tsp. baking soda |
| 1 egg | 1 tsp. salt |
| ¼ tsp. lemon extract | ½ c. finely chopped, |
| 1 (8½ oz.) can | pitted dates |
| crushed pineapple | ¼ c. water |
| ¼ c. chopped nuts | ¼ c. chopped |
| 2½ c. sifted flour | maraschino cherries |

• Cream butter and sugar; add egg and lemon extract. Drain pineapple, reserving liquid. Add crushed pineapple and nuts to creamed mixture.
• Sift dry ingredients together. Add dates and mix well, separating date pieces with your fingers. Stir dry ingredients into creamed mixture alternately with reserved pineapple juice plus ¼ c. water. Fold in the chopped maraschino cherries. Pour into greased 9×5×3″ loaf pan. Bake in 375° oven about 55 minutes. Cool in pan 10 minutes. Remove from pan; cool. Makes about 10 servings.

## Peachy Oatmeal Bread

*Makes a delightful dessert on a cold winter night*

| | |
|---|---|
| 1¾ c. sifted flour | ⅔ c. milk |
| ¾ c. sugar | 1 egg, slightly beaten |
| 4½ tsp. baking powder | ½ c. melted butter |
| ¾ tsp. salt | 1 (1 lb. 14 oz.) can |
| 1½ tsp. ground | cling peach halves, |
| cinnamon | well drained |
| ¾ tsp. ground nutmeg | ⅓ c. brown sugar, |
| ¼ tsp. ground cloves | firmly packed |
| 1½ c. quick rolled oats | 3 tblsp. melted butter |
| ½ c. chopped nuts | |

• Sift together flour, sugar, baking powder, salt and spices. Stir in oats and nuts.
• Combine milk, egg and ½ c. melted butter. Stir into dry ingredients until moistened. Do not beat. Pour batter into greased 8×8×2″ baking pan.
• Bake in 375° oven 40 to 45 minutes.
• Freeze if you wish. Defrost and add topping just before serving.

**Topping:** Chop or slice peaches. Arrange on cooled bread. Sprinkle with brown sugar; dribble 3 tblsp. melted butter on top. Broil 4″ from the broiler unit until topping bubbles, and tops of peaches begin to brown. Makes about 9 servings.

## Orange Prune Coffee Bread

*Cut into thin slices and spread with cream cheese*

| | |
|---|---|
| 2 eggs | 4 c. biscuit mix |
| ½ c. brown sugar, | 1 tsp. baking soda |
| firmly packed | 1½ c. chopped, |
| ½ c. sugar | pitted prunes |
| 3 tblsp. finely shredded | 1⅓ c. fresh orange |
| orange rind | juice |

• Beat eggs well; stir in sugars and orange rind.
• Combine biscuit mix and soda. Add chopped prunes and mix well, separating prune pieces with your fingers. Stir into sugar mixture alternately with orange juice. Beat by hand for 1 minute; do not overbeat. Pour into a greased 10″ fluted tube pan or 10″ tube pan.
• Bake in 350° oven 45 minutes or until bread tests done in center. Cool 10 minutes. Remove from pan and cool completely. Makes 12 to 16 servings.

A trio of quick breads that can be frozen ahead for holiday gift-giving. Thaw and wrap in colored foil; tie with bright ribbon. We feature Orange Prune Coffee Bread (top); Pineapple Date Loaf (center) and Peachy Oatmeal Bread.

# Pickled vegetables

**A** good country meal is not complete without at least one homemade relish. Often two or three pickles or relish dishes add interest to the menu—sometimes take the place of salad. The pickled vegetables pictured here are a perfect gourmet gift for someone who "has everything." They can be made a few weeks ahead and refrigerated. They are perfect go-alongs with meat and poultry. And they make dramatic garnishes too: Wreathe the holiday turkey with Pickled Cherry Tomatoes. Surround a roast pork with Sweet Pickled Carrots or a glistening baked ham with the Dilled Green Beans. Pass a dish of Pickled Green Peppers to accompany a pot of homemade baked beans. For a really luxurious special gift, pack one of each of the pickled beauties in a pretty wicker basket.

### Sweet Pickled Carrots

*Makes the perfect hostess gift tied with a ribbon*

| | |
|---|---|
| 18 medium carrots, pared and cut in diagonal slices | 2 c. sugar |
| | 2 c. water |
| | 1 tsp. salt |
| 2 medium onions, cut in rings | 1 tsp. ground allspice |
| | 1 tsp. ground cloves |
| 2 c. vinegar | 1 stick cinnamon |

• Cook carrots and onion in boiling salted water until almost tender (about 8 minutes). Drain well.
• Combine remaining ingredients and bring to a boil in a saucepan. Meanwhile pack carrots and onion rings in hot jars.
• Pour on hot syrup. Seal; store in refrigerator. Should keep for a few months. (Do not store at room temperature.) Makes about 4 pints.

### Pickled Green Peppers

*Relish develops to full flavor in five weeks*

| | |
|---|---|
| 9 large green peppers, seeded and cut in eighths | 6 c. vinegar |
| | 1½ c. water |
| | 1½ c. sugar |
| 3 sprigs parsley | 1 tblsp. salt |
| 3 cloves garlic | 1 tblsp. olive oil |
| 3 slices anchovies | |

Photography/Chas. P. Mills & Son

Homemade pickled vegetables make lovely hostess gifts. Just pack into jars and refrigerate a month or so before the holidays. We feature, starting right front (clockwise): Dilled Green Beans, Sweet Pickled Carrots, Pickled Green Peppers, Dilled Green Beans and Pickled Cherry Tomatoes.

• Pack green peppers, 1 sprig parsley, 1 clove garlic and 1 slice anchovy in each hot jar.
• Heat remaining ingredients to boiling. Pour into jars. Seal; store in refrigerator. Should keep for a few months. (Do not store at room temperature.) Makes about 3 quarts.

### Dilled Green Beans

*A very special treat for your next annual reunion*

| | |
|---|---|
| 9 lbs. green beans | 2 qts. water |
| Fresh garlic cloves | 1 qt. cider vinegar |
| Fresh dill weed | ¾ tsp. salt |

• Wash beans and cut off ends. Cook beans in boiling water for 10 minutes. Blanch in cold water. Pack beans, garlic and dill weed in hot jars.
• Combine water, vinegar and salt in a saucepan. Bring to a boil. Pour over beans in jars. Seal; store in refrigerator. Should keep for a few months. (Do not store at room temperature.) Makes 7 quarts.

### Pickled Cherry Tomatoes

*This colorful relish will complement any meal*

| | |
|---|---|
| 2 pts. red cherry tomatoes | 2 tblsp. dill seed |
| | 2 c. vinegar |
| 2 stalks celery, sliced | 1 tsp. salt |
| 1 green pepper, cut in strips | 1 qt. water |

• Wash and stem cherry tomatoes. Pack in hot jars with celery, green pepper, and dill seed.
• Heat remaining ingredients to boiling; boil for 5 minutes. Pour into jars. Seal; store in refrigerator. Should keep for a few months. (Do not store at room temperature.) Makes 4 pints.

# Homemade cookies

You'll like these two scrumptious cookies—pack them as gifts, share with neighbors, or pass along with punch or coffee when friends drop in to say hello. One is a golden sugar cookie with the slightest hint of lemon. It has swirls of marmalade over the icing for a party touch. The other is a rich spicy pumpkin bar spread with a smooth creamy icing and topped with a pecan half. Both can be made ahead and tucked in the freezer.

### Danish Sugar Cookies

*Serve these handsome cookies with ice cream sundaes*

| | |
|---|---|
| ½ c. butter | 2 c. sifted flour |
| ½ c. shortening | ½ tsp. baking soda |
| 1 c. sugar | ½ tsp. cream of tartar |
| 1 egg | ⅛ tsp. salt |
| ½ tsp. vanilla | Sugar |
| ½ tsp. lemon extract | |

• Cream together butter, shortening and sugar until light and fluffy. Add egg, vanilla and lemon extract; beat well.
• Sift together next 4 ingredients. Stir gradually into creamed mixture. Chill well.
• Shape dough into 1″ balls and roll in sugar. Place 1″ apart on greased baking sheet. Flatten by pressing with bottom of drinking glass.
• Bake in 350° oven 10 minutes or until golden. Cool on racks. Makes about 5 dozen.

If you wish, frost cookies with your favorite confectioners sugar icing. Top with swirls of red raspberry or apricot preserves which have been thinned with light corn syrup.

### Spicy Pumpkin Bars

*So good served with steaming mugs of apple cider*

| | |
|---|---|
| ½ c. shortening | 1¼ tsp. ground cinnamon |
| 1 c. brown sugar, firmly packed | 1 tsp. ground nutmeg |
| ¼ c. sugar | 1 tsp. ground ginger |
| 4 eggs | ½ tsp. salt |
| 2 c. canned pumpkin | Cream Cheese Icing (recipe follows) |
| 2 c. sifted flour | |
| 4 tsp. baking powder | |

• Cream together shortening and sugars until light and fluffy. Add eggs, one at a time, beating well after each addition. Beat in pumpkin.
• Sift together dry ingredients. Gradually stir into creamed mixture. Spread batter in greased 15½ × 10½ × 1″ jelly roll pan.
• Bake in 350° oven 30 minutes or until it tests done. Cool in pan on rack. Spread with Cream Cheese Icing. If you wish, sprinkle with chopped walnuts or top with pecan halves. Cut into 3½ × 1¼″ bars. Makes 32.

**Cream Cheese Icing:** Combine 1 (3 oz.) pkg. softened cream cheese, 1 tblsp. butter, 2½ c. sifted confectioners sugar, 1 tsp. grated lemon rind, pinch salt and 1 tblsp. milk. Blend well.

# Two quick and easy candies

Children will have fun helping to make these candies—not just to eat but to give as gifts. Their pride in sharing something they have made is a satisfying experience. Alternate the chocolate covered peanut butter balls and the crunchy nut and cereal candy in a gift box. They look so pretty together.

## Chocolate Peanut Butter Balls

*These elegant candies do not require any cooking*

2 c. sifted confectioners sugar
1 c. peanut butter
¾ c. graham cracker crumbs

½ c. soft butter
6 (1 oz.) squares unsweetened chocolate
2½″ square paraffin

• Combine confectioners sugar, peanut butter, graham cracker crumbs and butter; mix until well blended. Roll into ¾″ balls. Chill for 1 hour.

• Coarsely chop chocolate and paraffin. Place in double boiler top over simmering water. Heat, stirring occasionally, until melted. Remove from heat, but leave double boiler top over water.

• Using a fork, dip balls in chocolate quickly. Let excess chocolate drip off. Place on waxed paper on baking sheets. Leave plain or press a peanut half on top of each. (They can also be rolled in chopped peanuts immediately after dipping.) Store in cool place. Makes about 4 dozen.

## Caramel Corn Flake Snacks

*Crisp and sweet, these candies will appeal to all*

1 (14 oz.) bag caramels
¼ c. milk
1 c. salted Spanish peanuts

6 c. corn flakes
Red candied cherries, halved

• Place caramels and milk in a double boiler top. Place over simmering water. Heat, stirring occasionally, until melted (about 25 minutes).

• Gradually pour mixture over combined peanuts and corn flakes in a large bowl, tossing quickly until well coated. Drop by tablespoonfuls onto waxed paper. Top each with a candied cherry half. Makes about 2 dozen.

# Christmas is sharing

# Jewel of a gift

Buy an antique glass container and give two presents in one. . . sparkling homemade jelly in a beautiful heirloom!

## Tangy Grapefruit Jelly

*Spoon this golden jelly over piping hot popovers*

| | |
|---|---|
| 3 c. canned or bottled grapefruit juice | 4 c. sugar |
| 1 pkg. powdered fruit pectin | 7 drops yellow food color |

• Combine grapefruit juice and powdered fruit pectin in large saucepan; mix well. Bring to a hard boil over high heat, stirring constantly. Stir in sugar all at once. Bring to a full rolling boil and boil 1 minute, stirring constantly. Remove from heat. Stir in food color. Skim.

• Ladle into hot, sterilized glasses. Cover immediately with ⅛″ hot paraffin. Makes 5 cups.

## Refreshing Lime Jelly

*Serve in lemon cups with crisp broiled chicken*

| | |
|---|---|
| 1 c. lime juice (about 6 limes) or bottled lime juice | 1 pkg. powdered fruit pectin |
| 2½ c. water | 5 c. sugar |
| | 6 drops green food color |

• Combine lime juice and water in large saucepan. Add powdered fruit pectin; mix well. Bring to a hard boil over high heat, stirring constantly. Stir in sugar all at once. Bring to a full rolling boil and boil 1 minute, stirring constantly. Remove from heat. Stir in food color. Skim.

• Ladle into hot, sterilized glasses. Cover immediately with ⅛″ hot paraffin. Makes 5 cups.

## Sparkling Cherry Jelly

*So good with peanut butter on crunchy saltines*

| | |
|---|---|
| 2 c. canned or bottled cherry drink | ½ bottle liquid fruit pectin |
| 3½ c. sugar | ¼ tsp. almond extract |
| 2 tblsp. lemon juice | 4 drops red food color |

• Combine cherry drink, sugar and lemon juice in large saucepan; mix well. Bring to a hard boil over high heat, stirring constantly. At once stir in pectin. Bring to a full rolling boil and boil 1 minute, stirring constantly. Remove from heat. Stir in almond extract and food color. Skim.

• Ladle into hot, sterilized glasses. Cover immediately with ⅛″ hot paraffin. Makes 5 cups.

# Four heirloom Christmas dinners

If you could take a trip around the USA during the Chistmas season and visit homes in every town and village, you'd find atremendous variety of holiday foods and customs—some old, some new and in each home a little different.

The first settlers in our land clung strongly to the traditions of the "old country," but as the generations passed and times changed, many of the customs and recipes were adapted to newer methods and different regional ingredients.

Today's generation may or may not remember great grandmother and her customs, but all over the country, families are reaching back to the past. There's a strong urge to return to solid comforting roots and to learn more about our origins. And with this interest, many of the old-time customs and wonderful homemade dishes inherited from our ancestors are coming back.

For those of Swedish descent the spicy smell of gingerbread and the lovely fragrance of saffron bread baking in the oven are reminiscent of an Old-world tradition. For Italian-Americans there are fond memories in the crisp light-as-air pastry strips veiled in powdered sugar. The fruit-filled fat stollens from Germany and the blazing plum puddings from England are still a very important part of our traditional American holiday feasting.

Today's homemakers are digging out recipes given to them as part of their heritage. They add them to their family's traditional Christmas to create a wonderfu mix of the old and the new.

So as a way of sharing in these delicious "melting pot" holiday cuisines, why not delight your family and friends with some heritage foods in addition to your own seasonal favorites.

On the following pages we feature four menus borrowed from Pennsylvania Dutch, German-, Italian- and Swedish-Americans. And along with this gala food, you'll find easy and imaginative ideas to give your entertaining an authentic setting.

# German trim-the-tree supper

## MENU

*Sauerbraten with Gingersnap Gravy\**
*Potato Dumplings\**
*Red Cabbage with Apples\**
*Homemade Applesauce*
*Rye Bread\**
*Individual Schaum Tortes with*
*Strawberries and Cream\**

*\*See recipes*

A hearty German-style feast to share with friends during the Christmas season. Left to right: homemade applesauce, sweet and sour Red Cabbage with Apples, Rye Bread, Sauerbraten with tender Potato Dumplings and rich Cream Gravy, spiced just right with crushed gingersnaps.

Photography/Richard Tomlinson    Photo Stylist/Sylvia Stern

The Germans brought their warm nostalgic Christmas traditions with them to America—along with sweet almond marzipan, brightly colored and shaped into fruits, vegetables and the traditional chubby pink pig.

Their Christmas tree often reaches to the ceiling. And shiny red apples along with gilded nuts and hand carved ornaments are as traditional to the Germans' tannenbaum as are strings of cranberries and popcorn to most Americans. There are greens everywhere—huge decorative swags of pine boughs over doorways, mirrors and pictures—and sweet scent fills the air.

As gifts are stacked in individual heaps on tables, rather than under the tree, tangy sweet-sour smells drift from the kitchen. Red cabbage simmers to perfection; puffy potato dumplings bubble gently in a kettle, and plump loaves of rye bread cool on racks.

After a hearty trim-the-tree supper, the gaily wrapped gifts are unwrapped and festive songs enrich the holiday mood.

So during this holiday season why not serve your own Sentimentally German Supper on the night you trim the tree—invite a few friends, too—and make it a real sharing experience.

## Individual Schaum Tortes with Strawberries and Cream

*Crisp on the outside; soft on the inside*

| | |
|---|---|
| 8 egg whites | 3 (10 oz.) pkgs. frozen |
| ½ tsp. cream of tartar | strawberries, thawed |
| 2 c. sugar | 2 c. heavy cream, |
| 1 tsp. vanilla | whipped and |
| 1 tsp. vinegar | sweetened |

• Beat egg whites in large bowl with electric mixer at high speed until frothy. Add cream of tartar; beat until egg whites are almost dry.
• Slowly add sugar, 2 tblsp. at a time, beating well after each addition. (Total beating time: 20 minutes.) Add vanilla and vinegar; beat 2 minutes. (Mixture should be very stiff and glossy.) Drop mixture by spoonfuls onto greased baking sheets, making 10 tortes.
• Bake in 250° oven 1 hour 15 minutes or until pale brown and crusty. Remove from baking sheets; cool on racks.

**To serve:** Spoon strawberries over each torte and top with whipped cream. Makes 10 servings.

## Rye Bread

*Perfect accompaniment to a German feast*

| | |
|---|---|
| 2 c. rye flour | ½ c. lukewarm water |
| ¾ c. dark molasses | 6½ c. sifted flour |
| ⅓ c. shortening | 1 egg white, slightly |
| 2 tsp. salt | beaten |
| 2 c. boiling water | 1 tblsp. water |
| 1 pkg. active dry yeast | Caraway seeds |

• Combine rye flour, molasses, shortening and salt in bowl. Stir in 2 c. boiling water. Cool to lukewarm.
• Sprinkle yeast on ½ c. lukewarm water; stir to dissolve. Add yeast and 1 c. flour to rye mixture. Beat with electric mixer at medium speed until smooth, about 2 mintues, scraping bowl occasionally. Or beat with spoon until batter is smooth.
• Gradually add remaining flour to make a soft dough that leaves the sides of the bowl. Turn onto lightly floured surface and knead until smooth and satiny, about 8 to 10 minutes.
• Place in lightly greased bowl; turn dough over to grease top. Cover and let rise in warm place until doubled, about 1 to 1½ hours.
• Divide dough in thirds. Shape into round loaves and place on greased baking sheets. Let rise until doubled. Brush with combined egg white and water. Sprinkle with caraway seeds.
• Bake in 350° oven 40 minutes or until loaves sound hollow when tapped. Remove from baking sheets. Cool on racks. Makes 3 loaves.

## Sauerbraten with Cream Gravy

*Marinating develops its sweet-sour flavor*

| | |
|---|---|
| 1 medium onion, sliced | 1 c. chopped onion |
| 1 c. cider vinegar | 1 c. chopped carrot |
| 2 c. water | ½ c. chopped celery |
| 2½ tsp. salt | 1 c. water |
| 12 whole peppercorns | 1 beef bouillon cube |
| 6 whole cloves | 1 c. water |
| 3 bay leaves | ¼ c. flour |
| 1 (5 lb.) boneless | ½ c. cold water |
| bottom round, rolled | ½ c. crushed ginger- |
| and tied | snaps |
| ¼ c. cooking oil | |

• Combine sliced onion, vinegar, 2 c. water, salt, peppercorns, cloves and bay leaves. Pour over roast in large glass dish, turning roast to coat all sides.

Cover and refrigerate 2 days, turning meat twice daily.
- Remove meat from marinade; dry with paper towels. Reserve 2 c. marinade. Brown meat on all sides in hot oil in Dutch oven, about 15 minutes. Remove meat. Add 1 c. onion, carrot and celery. Saute until tender (do not brown).
- Return meat to Dutch oven. Add reserved marinade and 1 c. water. Bring mixture to a boil. Reduce heat; cover and simmer 3 hours or until meat is tender.
- Remove meat to hot platter. Add bouillon cube and 1 c. water to Dutch oven. Bring mixture to a boil.
- Combine flour and ½ c. cold water; stir to blend. Gradually add to hot liquid, stirring constantly. Stir in gingersnaps. Bring mixture to a boil, stirring constantly. Boil 3 minutes. Serve gravy with sauerbraten. Makes 8 to 12 servings.

## Potato Dumplings

*A tradition with German sauerbraten*

| | |
|---|---|
| 5 c. seasoned mashed potatoes | 2 slices bread, toasted and cut in ¼" cubes |
| 1 c. sifted flour | Chopped fresh parsley |
| 1 egg | |

- Combine potatoes, flour and egg in bowl; mix well. Divide mixture into 12 portions, about ⅓ c. each. Shape each into a ball placing a few toast cubes in center.
- Drop dumplings in boiling salted water in Dutch oven. (Do not let water boil too hard or dumplings will break up.) Cook 10 to 12 minutes or until dumplings rise to surface of water. Boil 1 minute more. Remove with slotted spoon. Place around sauerbraten. Sprinkle dumplings with parsley. Makes 12 servings.

## Red Cabbage with Apples

*Typical dish simmered to tangy perfection*

| | |
|---|---|
| 1 medium head red cabbage, cut in ⅛" strips | 2 tblsp. butter or regular margarine |
| | ½ c. red wine vinegar |
| 2 medium apples, pared, cored and cut in ⅛" slices | 1 bay leaf |
| | 2 tblsp. sugar |
| ½ c. chopped onion | ½ tsp. salt |

- Cook cabbage, apples and onion in melted butter in large skillet or Dutch oven 5 minutes, stirring often to prevent sticking.
- Add vinegar, bay leaf, sugar and salt. Bring mixture to a boil. Reduce heat; cover and simmer 35 minutes or until cabbage is tender. Makes 8 to 12 servings.

## Bavarian Apple Strudel

*Also delicious made with cherry pie filling*

| | |
|---|---|
| 1 tblsp. cooking oil | 1 c. raisins |
| 1 egg, beaten | ¼ c. sugar |
| ⅓ c. lukewarm water | 1 tsp. ground cinnamon |
| ¼ tsp. salt | ⅓ c. melted butter or regular margarine |
| 1 ½ c. sifted flour | |
| 8 c. sliced, pared tart apples | ⅓ c. dry bread crumbs |
| | Confectioners sugar |

- Combine oil, egg, water and salt. Gradually add flour, beating with spoon until a firm dough that pulls away from the sides of the bowl is formed.
- Knead dough on floured surface until smooth and elastic, 5 minutes. Cover; let rest 30 minutes.
- Combine apples, raisins, sugar and cinnamon.
- Divide dough in half. Roll each half into 18 × 12" rectangle, stretching dough if necessary to make it very thin. Brush with melted butter. Sprinkle with half of bread crumbs. Spread half of apple mixture lengthwise in center third of dough. Fold dough over apples on one side and then the other. Brush with melted butter. Place on greased baking sheet. Repeat with remaining dough.
- Bake in 400° oven 30 minutes or until golden and apples are tender. Serve warm or cold sprinkled with confectioners sugar. Makes 16 servings.

## Pears and Potatoes

*This dish improves in flavor when reheated*

| | |
|---|---|
| 4 strips bacon, diced | 4 medium pears, pared and sliced |
| 3½ c. thickly sliced, pared potatoes | ¼ c. vinegar |
| 1 tsp. salt | 1 bay leaf |
| 1 c. hot water | ¼ tsp. ground allspice |

- Fry bacon in Dutch oven until crisp. Remove and drain on paper towels. Crumble and set aside.
- Add potatoes, salt and water to bacon drippings. Cover and bring to a boil; reduce heat and simmer 25 minutes or until potatoes are tender.
- Add pears, vinegar, bay leaf, allspice and reserved bacon. Cover and simmer 15 more minutes or until pears are tender. Makes 6 servings.

A do-ahead Italian-style supper. From left: tossed green salad, bread sticks, Antipasto, Ravioli with Sausage-Tomato Sauce, Deep-Fried Italian Pastries and a bowl of fresh fruit. To carry out the Italian theme, we chose the bright colors of their flag, red, green and yellow, to decorate the buffet table.

Photography/Richard Tomlinson    Photo Stylist/Sylvia Stern

# Italian-inspired Christmas week dinner

---

### MENU

---

*Antipasto\**
*Ravioli with Sausage-Tomato Sauce\**
*Tossed Green Salad*
*Bread Sticks*
*Creamy Grapefruit Sherbet\**
*Deep-Fried Italian Pastries\**

\*See recipes

In Italy, the Christmas celebrations vary with the regions. The north is famous for huge Christmas trees; the south is renowned for the Crib of Nativity. And in some regions, such as Tuscany, a huge log burns in the fireplace throughout the Yuletide family festivities.

An Italian-American Christmas is still very much a family affair, with gatherings limited to intimate friends and relatives. In preparation, the women are happily bustling around the kitchen making all kinds of good things to eat. Homemade pasta is rolled tissue thin. . . tomato sauce scented with herbs simmers in a big kettle. . . delicate pastries bubble in hot fat. . . plump chickens are gently simmering for basic golden broth.

A typical Christmas-week feast starts with a bowl of rich broth, followed by a portion of ravioli—little cushions of pasta stuffed with the family's favorite meat filling—and topped off with either chicken or turkey with a moist chestnut stuffing. And for a must during the season—Italians serve strufoli and frappe, ribbons and bows of sweet pastry—deep-fat fried in olive oil, drained, then dusted with confectioners sugar—so light they seem to almost blow away with each tasty bite.

For a fun way to entertain during the holidays, serve our Italian-inspired Christmas Week Dinner to an intimate gathering of family and friends. To make it easy for you, several of the dishes can be made ahead, and the antipasto tray can be whipped together in just a few seconds.

## Antipasto

*Traditional Italian first course*

| | |
|---|---|
| 1 lb. thinly sliced Italian ham | 24 radish roses |
| 1 lb. thinly sliced Italian salami | 24 pimiento-stuffed green olives |
| 6 hard-cooked eggs, cut in quarters | 2 tomatoes, cut in wedges |
| 2 bunches scallions, washed and trimmed | Marinated Mushrooms (recipe follows) |

• Roll ham and salami into small rolls. Arrange the meat and the rest of the ingredients in an attractive design on a large platter or serving tray. Cover with plastic wrap and refrigerate until serving time. Serve as an appetizer. Makes 8 to 12 servings.

**Marinated Mushrooms:** Combine ⅔ c. salad oil, ⅓ c. wine vinegar, ¼ c. water, 1 bay leaf, 6 peppercorns, ½ tsp. salt and 2 cloves garlic, halved, in 12″ skillet. Bring mixture to a boil. Reduce heat; cover and simmer 15 minutes. Uncover.
• Add 1 medium onion, thinly sliced, and 1 lb. fresh mushrooms, sliced. Simmer 5 minutes, stirring often. Remove from heat. Cool.
• Store in covered container in refrigerator. (Will keep for 2 days.) Makes 8 to 12 servings.

## Creamy Grapefruit Sherbet

*So good with crisp Italian pastries*

| | |
|---|---|
| 1½ c. canned or fresh grapefruit juice | 1 egg, separated |
| ¾ c. sugar | 1 c. heavy cream |
| ¾ c. orange juice | ⅛ tsp. salt |
| 2 tsp. grated orange rind | ¼ c. sugar |

• Combine grapefruit juice and ¾ c. sugar in saucepan. Heat until sugar is dissolved. Remove from heat. Add orange juice and orange rind. Pour into 9×5×3″ loaf pan. Freeze until mushy.
• Beat egg yolk until lemon colored; set aside.
• Whip heavy cream until thickened. Gradually beat in salt, ¼ c. sugar and beaten egg yolk.
• Beat egg white until stiff peaks form. Fold into whipped cream.
• Stir mushy grapefruit mixture into whipped cream. Pour into loaf pan. Freeze until sherbet is frozen ¼″ around sides of loaf pan, about 30 minutes. Remove sherbet from pan and stir well. Return to loaf pan. Cover with foil. Freeze completely. Makes 8 to 12 servings.

## Deep-Fried Italian Pastries

*These pastry knots keep well in a covered container*

| | |
|---|---|
| 2 c. sifted flour | 1 tsp. rum flavoring |
| ⅛ tsp. salt | ¼ c. sifted flour |
| 3 eggs | Cooking oil |
| 1 tblsp. milk | Confectioners sugar |

• Place 2 c. flour in bowl. Make a well in center. Add salt, eggs, milk and rum flavoring. Mix well with fork just until moistened. Shape into a ball.
• Sprinkle ¼ c. flour on board. Knead dough on board until smooth and shiny, about 10 minutes. Wrap in plastic wrap; refrigerate at least 1 hour.

- Divide dough in fourths. Roll each out on floured surface to 13 × 11" rectangle. Cut into 13 × 1" strips. Tie each strip into a loose knot.
- Pour cooking oil into deep-fat fryer or large skillet, filling one-third full. Heat to 350°. Fry knots, 4 or 5 at a time, 1 to 2 minutes or until golden brown. Drain on paper towels. Sprinkle with confectioners sugar. Store in large covered container. Makes 44 pastries.

## Ravioli with Sausage-Tomato Sauce

*Homemade pasta is well worth the time and effort*

| | |
|---|---|
| 1½ lbs. Italian pork sausage links, cut in chunks | 1 tsp. sugar |
| 2 tblsp. cooking oil | ¼ c. finely chopped green pepper |
| 1 c. chopped onion | 3 c. sifted flour |
| 2 cloves garlic, minced | ½ tsp. salt |
| 2 bay leaves | 2 eggs, beaten |
| 3 tsp. dried oregano leaves | ½ c. warm water |
| 1 tsp. dried basil leaves | 1 c. ricotta cheese |
| 1 tsp. salt | 1 egg, beaten |
| ¼ tsp. pepper | ¼ c. grated Parmesan cheese |
| 2 (2 lb. 3 oz.) cans Italian-style tomatoes | 1 tblsp. minced fresh parsley |
| 2 (15 oz.) cans tomato sauce | ⅛ tsp. salt |
| | Dash of pepper |
| | Chopped fresh parsley |

- Lightly brown pork sausage in hot oil in Dutch oven. Pour off drippings, reserving 2 tblsp. Add onion, garlic, bay leaves, oregano, basil, 1 tsp. salt and ¼ tsp. pepper. Cook until meat mixture is well browned.
- Blend tomatoes in blender until smooth. Add tomatoes, tomato sauce, sugar and green pepper to Dutch oven. Bring to a boil. Reduce heat and simmer 50 minutes.
- Sift together flour and ½ tsp. salt on board. Make a deep impression in mound; pour in 2 eggs. Mix eggs into flour by folding and lifting with hands until well mixed. Gradually add warm water and start shaping into a ball. Knead dough a few minutes. Add more water if dough seems dry. Shape into a ball. Cover with a bowl. Let stand 15 minutes.
- Knead dough a few more minutes or until it becomes smooth and air pockets disappear. Cover with bowl. Let stand 15 minutes. Repeat again.
- Combine ricotta cheese, 1 egg, Parmesan cheese, 1 tblsp. parsley, ⅛ tsp. salt and dash of pepper; mix until well blended. Set aside.
- Divide dough in quarters. Roll one quarter into large rectangle making the dough as thin as possible. Trim with pastry wheel or knife to 12 × 8" rectangle. Using dull side of knife so as not to cut through dough, divide rectangle into 24 (2") squares. Place a teaspoonful of ricotta filling in center of each square. Cover with damp paper towel.
- Roll another quarter of dough into large rectangle, making the dough as thin as possible. Trim to 13 × 9" rectangle. Cover with damp paper towel.
- Brush water on lines between mounds of filling and around edges of first rectangle. Quickly lay second rectangle on top, pressing down between mounds to seal. Cut squares apart with pastry wheel or knife. Cover with damp paper towel. Repeat procedure with remaining dough and filling.
- Drop half of ravioli squares into 6 to 8 quarts rapidly boiling salted water. Boil 20 minutes or until tender. Stir gently occasionally to keep them from sticking. Remove with slotted spoon and drain well. Cook and drain remaining ravioli.
- Spread sauce in each of two 11 × 7 × 2" baking dishes. Place 12 ravioli in each dish; spread with sauce. Repeat layers dividing sauce between dishes. Cover with foil; refrigerate until ready to heat.
- Bake uncovered in 350° oven 50 minutes or until hot and bubbly. Garnish with chopped parsley. Makes 8 to 12 servings.

# Swedish-style
# holiday smorgasbord

Photography/Richard Tomlinson    Photo Stylist/Sylvia Stern

For Swedish-Americans, the Christmas spirit pervades for a whole month. They like an old-fashioned Christmas, with flickering candles on giant trees, homemade pastries and cookies of every description, roasted meats and lots of salads. Six weeks before Christmas, Swedish women bake all kinds of goodies to have a well-stocked larder—plenty of good food to offer friends during the joyous season.

Christmas Eve is the most important time for Swedes—the night when the most lavish meal of the whole Christmas season is served. On Christmas day itself, a cold buffet is featured, followed by other days of feasting with friends and neighbors.

The Swedish smorgasbord is a convenient and gracious way to entertain. Guests can help themselves from the buffet, laden with good food.

Delight your friends and family this season with our Swedish-style Holiday Smorgasbord—filled with good things to eat—right down to the traditional dessert, creamy rice pudding with almonds.

# MENU

*Swedish Meatballs with Sauce\**
*Herring and Beet Salad\**
*Fish Salad with Peas\**
*Pickled Cucumbers with Dill\**
*Assorted Crackers   Assorted Cheeses*
*Saffron Braid\**
*Almond-Rice Pudding\**
*Glogg\**

\*See recipes

A wonderful taste of Sweden. Left front: assorted cheeses, Saffron Braid, Fish Salad with Peas and Pickled Cucumbers with Dill. Left rear: Swedish Meatballs with Sauce, Almond-Rice Pudding, Glogg, and assorted crackers.

## Saffron Braid

*Saffron braid and Christmas go together in Sweden*

| | |
|---|---|
| 1 c. milk | ¼ c. lukewarm water |
| ½ c. sugar | 1 egg |
| 2 tblsp. butter or regular margarine | ½ tsp. ground cardamom |
| | 4¼ c. sifted flour |
| ½ tsp. salt | 1 egg, beaten |
| Pinch of saffron | Sugar |
| 1 pkg. active dry yeast | |

• Scald milk. Add to ½ c. sugar, butter, salt and saffron in bowl. Cool to lukewarm.

• Sprinkle yeast on lukewarm water; stir to dissolve. Add yeast, 1 egg, cardamom and 1 c. flour to milk mixture. Beat with electric mixer at medium speed until smooth, about 2 minutes, scraping bowl occasionally. Or beat with spoon until batter is smooth.

• Gradually add enough flour to make a soft dough that leaves the sides of the bowl. Turn out on floured surface and knead until smooth and satiny, about 10 minutes.

• Place dough in lightly greased bowl; turn over to grease top. Cover and let rise in warm place until doubled, about 1½ hours.

• Divide dough in half. Divide each half into thirds. Roll each third into a 10″ strip. Braid three strips together. Pinch ends to seal. Place on greased baking sheet. Let rise until doubled, about 1 hour.

• Brush braids with egg. Sprinkle with sugar.

• Bake in 375° oven 20 to 25 minutes or until loaves sound hollow when tapped. Remove from baking sheets; cool on racks. Makes 2 loaves.

## Almond-Rice Pudding

*This is the traditional Swedish dessert*

| | |
|---|---|
| 1¼ c. regular rice | 2 c. heavy cream |
| ⅔ c. sugar | Chopped red candied cherries |
| 1 tsp. salt | |
| 6 c. milk | Raspberry Sauce (recipe follows) |
| ⅓ c. cream sherry | |
| 3 tsp. vanilla | |
| 1⅓ c. toasted slivered almonds | |

• Combine rice, sugar, salt and milk in 3-qt. saucepan. Bring mixture to a boil over medium heat, stirring constantly. Reduce heat; simmer uncovered 25 minutes, stirring frequently. Remove from heat.

• Pour rice mixture into 13×9×2″ baking dish. Cool slightly. Stir in sherry, vanilla and almonds.

• Whip cream until soft peaks form. Fold into rice mixture. Cover. Chill several hours. Garnish with cherries. Serve with Raspberry Sauce. Makes 8 to 12 servings.

**Raspberry Sauce:** Combine 2 (10 oz.) pkgs. frozen raspberries, thawed, 2 tblsp. cornstarch and 2 tsp. lemon juice in a saucepan. Bring to a boil, stirring constantly. Boil 1 minute. Remove from heat. Strain. Cool.

## Glogg

*A spicy hot punch for the cold weather holidays*

| | |
|---|---|
| ½ c. sugar | Peel from 1 whole orange |
| 1 c. raisins | |
| 3 whole cardamom seeds, crushed | 3 c. dry red wine |
| | 1 c. port wine |
| 6 whole cloves | 1 c. Swedish aquavit or vodka |
| 1 stick cinnamon | |
| 1″ piece crystallized ginger | 1 c. blanched whole almonds |

• Combine sugar, raisins, cardamom, cloves, cinnamon, ginger, orange peel and wines in enamel or stainless steel saucepan. Let stand 3 hours.

• Add aquavit and almonds. Stir well. Bring mixture to a boil over high heat. Remove from heat. Serve at once. Makes 8 to 12 servings.

## Pickled Cucumbers with Dill

*Cucumber marinated in vinegar, garnished with dill*

| | |
|---|---|
| ½ c. vinegar | 2 medium cucumbers |
| ¼ c. sugar | 2 tsp. dried dill weed or 2 tblsp. chopped fresh dill |
| 2 tblsp. water | |
| ½ tsp. salt | |
| ⅛ tsp. pepper | |

• Combine vinegar, sugar, water, salt and pepper in saucepan. Bring to a boil. Remove from heat. Cool.

• Remove lengthwise strips of peel from cucumbers with vegetable peeler, leaving alternate strips of peel intact. Cut cucumbers in thin slices and place in bowl. Add vinegar mixture. Sprinkle with dill. Toss gently. Cover. Chill 2 to 3 hours. Makes 8 to 12 servings.

## Herring and Beet Salad

*One variation of this popular Swedish salad*

3 c. diced cooked
  beets
1 c. chopped pickled
  herring
½ c. diced cooked
  potatoes
½ c. diced dill pickle
½ c. chopped pared
  apples
⅓ c. finely chopped
  onion
3 tblsp. chopped
  fresh dill

2 tblsp. vinegar
¼ tsp. salt
⅛ tsp. pepper
3 hard-cooked eggs
2 tblsp. vinegar
1 tblsp. prepared
  yellow mustard
¼ c. salad oil
3 tblsp. heavy cream
1 tblsp. chopped
  fresh dill

• Combine beets, herring, potatoes, pickle, apples, onion, 3 tblsp. dill, 2 tblsp. vinegar, salt and pepper in bowl. Toss gently to mix.

• Remove yolks from eggs. Chop egg whites and reserve. Mash yolks with fork in bowl to a smooth paste. Add 2 tblsp. vinegar, mustard and oil; mix well. Stir in heavy cream; blend well. Pour over beet mixture. Toss gently. Cover. Chill at least 2 hours.

• Garnish salad with chopped egg whites and 1 tblsp. dill before serving. Makes 8 to 12 servings.

## Fish Salad with Peas

*This tasty salad has a zippy mustard dressing*

2 lbs. haddock fillets,
  cooked, drained
  and flaked
2 tblsp. lemon juice
2 tblsp. salad oil
2 c. cooked peas
2 tsp. lemon juice
2 tsp. salad oil
2 egg yolks, slightly
  beaten

1½ tsp. prepared
  yellow mustard
¾ tsp. salt
¼ tsp. pepper
1 tblsp. vinegar
¼ c. salad oil
⅓ c. melted butter or
  regular margarine

• Combine haddock, 2 tblsp. lemon juice and 2 tblsp. oil in bowl. Toss gently to mix. Cover with plastic wrap. Refrigerate.

• Combine peas, 2 tsp. lemon juice and 2 tsp. oil in bowl. Toss gently. Cover with plastic wrap. Chill.

• Combine egg yolks, mustard, salt, pepper, vinegar and ¼ c. oil in small saucepan. Stir in butter. Cook over low heat, stirring constantly, until mixture thickens. Cool well.

• Pour sauce over fish mixture. Toss gently to mix. Place fish salad in center of serving dish and surround with peas. Makes 8 to 12 servings.

## Swedish Meatballs with Sauce

*Serve these tiny meatballs in a chafing dish*

⅓ c. minced onion
2 tblsp. butter or regular
  margarine
1 lb. ground beef
1 c. unseasoned
  mashed potatoes
⅓ c. dry bread crumbs
1 tblsp. minced
  fresh parsley
1 tsp. salt
1 egg

¼ c. heavy cream
2 tblsp. butter or regular
  margarine
2 tblsp. cooking oil
2 tblsp. flour
¼ tsp. ground allspice
½ tsp. bottled browning
  sauce for gravy
1½ c. heavy cream
Chopped fresh parsley

• Saute onion in 2 tblsp. melted butter in small skillet until tender (do not brown). Set aside.

• Combine ground beef, potatoes, bread crumbs, 1 tblsp. parsley, salt, egg, ¼ c. heavy cream and sauteed onion. Mix until ingredients are well blended. Shape mixture into ¾″ meatballs. Arrange on a tray. Cover. Chill at least 1 hour.

• Brown 10 meatballs at a time in 2 tblsp. melted butter and oil in heavy 10″ skillet. Shake pan back and forth frequently to keep meatballs round. Add more oil if needed. Remove meatballs as they brown and place in 2-qt. casserole. Keep hot in 200° oven.

• Pour off all but 2 tblsp. pan drippings. Stir in flour, allspice and bottled sauce for gravy. Cook 1 minute, stirring constantly. Remove from heat. Slowly stir in heavy cream. Cook over low heat until slightly thickened. Pour over meatballs. Garnish with chopped parsley. Makes 8 to 12 servings.

## Swedish Pancakes

*Serve with whipped cream and plums for Christmas*

3 eggs
1¼ c. milk
¾ c. sifted flour
1 tblsp. sugar
½ tsp. salt

1 tsp. vanilla
Melted butter or regular
  margarine
Sugar

• Blend together eggs and milk with rotary beater. Add flour, 1 tblsp. sugar and salt; blend well.

• Bake in lightly greased 8″ skillet, using ¼ c. batter for each. (Tilt skillet back and forth quickly when batter is added to make a thin coating.) Bake until top is dry; turn and brown other side.

• Spread with melted butter and sprinkle with sugar. Roll up. Makes 8 pancakes.

A memorable Pennsylvania Dutch feast to share with family and friends: Roast Loin of Pork with Fried Apple Rings, Baked Onions, Turnips and Potatoes, Spinach and Mushroom Vinaigrette, Pickled Red Beet Eggs, Pepper Relish, Raised Muffins and Lemon Sponge Pie.

## MENU

*Roast Loin of Pork\**
*Fried Apple Rings\**
*Baked Onions\**
*Turnips and Potatoes\**
*Spinach and Mushroom Vinaigrette\**
*Pickled Red Beet Eggs\**
*Pepper Relish\**
*Raised Muffins\**
*Lemon Sponge Pie\**

°See recipes

# Pennsylvania Dutch Christmas feast

In Pennsylvania Dutch country, Christmas is a time for great family gatherings and tables groaning with food. Every room is decorated with greens and holly and usually there is a beautiful blue spruce Christmas tree that stretches to the ceiling.

At the beginning of the holiday season, the creche is unpacked and set up on a mantle bedecked with greens and candles. Many of these nativity scenes have been cherished for years and handed down through the generations.

Then the baking and food preparations begin. The foods are a combination of German foods and those grown on their Lancaster County land. Traditional Pennsylvania Dutch cooking is noted for its combination of "sweets and sours" that have been carefully selected to complement the meat. At every meal there will be at least two sours such as a relish and a pickle and two sweets, perhaps a preserve and a cake or pie.

It is not unusual to have a second Christmas dinner to accommodate the large number of relatives that come to visit. A favorite day-after-Christmas feast often features a crackling crisp Roast Loin of Pork and sugar-sparkled Fried Apple Slices for the main course. At every holiday meal a big bowl of Pickled Red Beet Eggs is a must. Turnips and Potatoes are traditionally served with pork along with Baked Onions. The finale of the meal is light and refreshing Lemon Sponge Pie.

For a change of pace, this would be a delicious dinner to serve on Christmas day instead of the conventional turkey and dressing.

## Roast Loin of Pork

*Succulent pork roast with glistening jelly glaze*

| | |
|---|---|
| 5 lbs. pork loin roast | Pepper |
| Salt | Apple jelly |

• Rub surface of pork roast with salt and pepper. Place roast on rack in roasting pan. Insert a meat thermometer in thickest part of roast. (Be sure it doesn't touch a bone.)
• Roast in 325° oven until done, allowing 30 minutes per pound. (Meat thermometer should read 185°.)
• During the last 30 minutes of roasting, brush pork loin frequently with melted apple jelly.
• Remove from oven. Let roast stand 20 minutes before carving. Makes 6 servings.

## Fried Apple Rings

*Place apple rings around pork roast for garnish*

| | |
|---|---|
| 3 large firm apples | 1 tblsp. sugar |
| 3 tblsp. butter or regular margarine | |

• Core apples, but do not pare. Slice apples in ¼″ rings.
• Melt butter in heavy skillet. Add apple slices; sprinkle with sugar. Cook over medium heat, turning apple rings when they are golden brown. Cook until tender. Makes 6 servings.

## Raised Muffins

*So light and feathery. . . excellent for dinner*

| | |
|---|---|
| 2 tblsp. butter or regular margarine | ¾ c. boiling water |
| ⅓ c. sugar | 1 pkg. active dry yeast |
| 1 tsp. salt | 1 egg, beaten |
| 1 c. milk, scalded | 3½ c. sifted flour |

• Combine butter, sugar, salt, milk and water. Cool to lukewarm.
• Sprinkle yeast over milk mixture; stir to dissolve. Add egg and flour; mix well. Cover and let rise in warm place until doubled, about 1½ hours.
• Spoon into greased muffin pan cups, filling ⅔ full. Let rise until batter comes to the top of pans.
• Bake in 375° oven 30 minutes or until golden brown. Makes 24 muffins.

## Turnips and Potatoes

*Chicken broth can also be used in this recipe*

| | |
|---|---|
| 1½ lbs. turnips | 1 tsp. salt |
| 1½ lbs. potatoes | ⅛ tsp. pepper |
| 2 c. pork broth | 2 tsp. chopped chives |

- Pare turnips and potatoes. Cut in ⅓″ slices.
- Place sliced vegetables, broth, salt, pepper and chives in Dutch oven. Cover. Bring to a boil; reduce heat and simmer 20 minutes or until vegetables are tender. Serve vegetables in the broth which can be mashed into them. Makes 6 servings.

## Spinach and Mushroom Vinaigrette

*Tangy salad dressing is perfect with fresh spinach*

| | |
|---|---|
| 1 lb. fresh spinach | 2 tblsp. vinegar |
| ¼ lb. fresh mushrooms, sliced | ¼ tsp. salt |
| | ½ tsp. onion salt |
| ¾ c. olive oil | Dash of pepper |
| 2 tblsp. red wine | |

- Wash and stem spinach. Break into bite-size pieces. Combine spinach and mushrooms in large bowl.
- Combine oil, red wine, vinegar, salt, onion salt and pepper in small jar. Cover and shake until well mixed. Pour oven spinach mixture; toss gently to mix. Serve immediately. Makes 6 servings.

## Pickled Red Beet Eggs

*This unusual relish is typically Pennsylvania Dutch*

| | |
|---|---|
| 1 lb. small firm beets, about 2″ diameter | ⅓ c. cider vinegar |
| | 6 hard-cooked eggs |
| 1 c. sugar | |

- Wash beets. Cook in boiling water to cover until tender, about 30 minutes. Remove beets and reserve cooking liquid.
- Remove beet skins and cut in ¼″ slices.
- Add sugar and vinegar to cooking liquid in pan. Stir until dissolved. Bring mixture to a boil. Add sliced beets and cook over low heat 5 minutes.
- Remove beets and strain cooking liquid into bowl or quart jar. Put eggs into cooking liquid, making sure they are completely covered. Top with beets. Cover and refrigerate at least 12 hours.
- Serve eggs whole or sliced with beets as a relish. Makes 6 servings.

## Pepper Relish

*Serve this colorful relish in a crystal dish*

| | |
|---|---|
| 1½ c. chopped red peppers | 2 c. sugar |
| | 1 c. cider vinegar |
| 1½ c. chopped green peppers | 2 tblsp. mustard seeds |
| | 1 tblsp. celery seeds |
| 1 c. chopped onion | 1 tsp. salt |
| 1 tsp. salt | |

- Combine peppers, onion and 1 tsp. salt in Dutch oven. Add water to cover. Bring to a boil; reduce heat and simmer until peppers are tender, but still crisp. Drain well.
- Combine sugar, vinegar, mustard seeds, celery seeds and 1 tsp. salt in 2-qt. saucepan. Bring to a boil, stirring until sugar is dissolved.
- Add drained pepper mixture. Bring to a boil; reduce heat and simmer 2 minutes. Ladle into hot, sterilized jars and seal. Makes 4 pints.

## Baked Onions

*Golden brown onions are a tasty accent to pork*

| | |
|---|---|
| 6 medium white onions | Salt |
| Melted butter or regular margarine | |

- Peel onions. Place in buttered 11×7×1½″ baking dish.
- Bake in 325° oven 1½ hours, basting with melted butter several times, until tender. Sprinkle baked onions with salt before serving. Makes 6 servings.

## Lemon Sponge Pie

*The perfect finale. . . delicately tangy lemon pie*

| | |
|---|---|
| 2 tblsp. shortening | 1 c. milk |
| 1 c. sugar | ¼ c. lemon juice |
| ½ tsp. salt | 1 tblsp. grated lemon peel |
| 3 tblsp. flour | |
| 2 eggs, separated | 1 (9″) unbaked pie shell |

- Cream together shortening, sugar and salt until light and fluffy. Add flour.
- Beat egg yolks; combine with milk, lemon juice and lemon peel. Add to creamed mixture; beat well.
- Beat egg whites until stiff peaks form. Fold into mixture. Pour into pie shell.
- Bake in 375° oven 10 minutes. Reduce oven temperature to 350° and continue baking 35 more minutes. Cool. Makes 6 servings.

# New turkey dishes

On the day after Christmas and all through the week, you can continue to feast gloriously on leftover turkey.

We've come up with some deliciously different recipes featuring turkey. Many of them are an adaptation of international recipes to lend a gourmet flavor. They are elegant enough to serve for any company meal.

If you like Italian food, make Golden Turkey Lasagne. Add a tossed green salad, toasted Italian bread and lemon sherbet for an interesting luncheon to serve drop-in guests.

And for those who like their food on the fiery side, try our exciting Turkey Curry with Rice (see photo) and Mexican Sour Cream Enchiladas. Either one of these is a perfect choice for make-ahead company meals.

In the mood for Chinese food? Then you'll like Cantonese Sweet and Sour Turkey—ladled over hot fluffy rice or crunchy noodles.

Hearty eaters will dig into the rib-sticking English Turkey Vegetable Pie; it's chock-full of colorful vegetables and rich creamy gravy.

Once you have sampled these deluxe turkey recipes, you'll never want to serve leftover turkey and warmed-over gravy again.

## Turkey Curry with Rice

*Pass several condiments to accent this curry dish*

| | |
|---|---|
| 1 c. sliced onion | 2 c. chicken broth |
| ¼ c. sliced carrots | 1 (4 oz.) can mushrooms |
| ¼ c. sliced celery | 3 c. cubed cooked |
| 1 apple, pared, cored | turkey |
| and sliced | 2 c. dairy sour cream |
| 1 clove garlic, minced | Hot fluffy rice |
| ¼ c. butter or regular | Condiments: Chopped |
| margarine | onions, raisins, cut |
| ⅓ c. flour | up green pepper, |
| 2½ tsp. curry powder | chopped tomato, |
| ¼ tsp. ground ginger | chopped hard-cooked |
| ¼ tsp. ground mace | eggs, chopped peanuts, |
| ¼ tsp. pepper | coconut and chutney |

• Saute onion, carrots, celery, apple and garlic in melted butter in 12″ skillet until tender (do not brown).
• Slowly blend in flour, curry powder, ginger, mace and pepper. Gradually add chicken broth and undrained mushrooms. Cook over medium heat, stirring constantly, until mixture thickens. Bring to a boil. Reduce heat; simmer 5 minutes.
• Stir in turkey. Heat 8 minutes more. Stir in sour cream. Heat 2 minutes more. Serve with rice. Pass selection of assorted Condiments. Makes 6 servings.

## Cantonese Sweet and Sour Turkey

*An oriental-inspired dish featuring a pungent sauce*

| | |
|---|---|
| 1 (1 lb. 4 oz.) can pine- | 1¼ c. green pepper |
| apple chunks | strips |
| ½ c. brown sugar, firmly | 1 c. sliced onion |
| packed | 1 c. sliced carrots |
| ¼ c. cornstarch | 2 c. cubed cooked |
| ½ tsp. ground ginger | turkey |
| ½ c. cider vinegar | Hot fluffy rice |
| ¼ c. soy sauce | |

• Drain pineapple; reserve juice. Add enough water to juice to make 3 c.
• Combine brown sugar, cornstarch and ginger in 10″ skillet. Gradually stir in pineapple juice, vinegar and soy sauce. Bring mixture to a boil, stirring constantly. Add pineapple, green pepper, onion, carrots and turkey. Bring mixture to a boil. Reduce heat; cover and simmer 10 minutes or until vegetables are tender-crisp. Serve with rice. Makes 6 servings.

## Turkey and Stuffing Scallop

*Moist stuffing and turkey topped with rich custard*

| | |
|---|---|
| 1 (8 oz.) pkg. herb- | ½ c. flour |
| seasoned stuffing mix | ¼ tsp. salt |
| ¾ c. chicken broth | ⅛ tsp. pepper |
| ¼ c. melted butter or | 4 c. chicken broth |
| regular margarine | 6 eggs, slightly beaten |
| 3 c. cubed cooked | Mushroom-Pimiento |
| turkey | Sauce (recipe |
| ½ c. butter or regular | follows) |
| margarine | |

• Combine stuffing mix, ¾ c. chicken broth and ¼ c. butter; mix well. Press mixture in greased 13×9×2″ baking dish. Top with layer of turkey.
• Melt ½ c. butter in 3-qt. saucepan. Stir in flour, salt and pepper. Cook over low heat, stirring constantly, until mixture is smooth and bubbly. Remove from heat. Stir in 4 c. chicken broth. Return to heat and cook over medium heat, stirring constantly, until mixture comes to a boil. Remove from heat. Add some of hot mixture to eggs; stir well. Slowly stir egg mixture into the hot mixture. Pour over turkey in baking dish.
• Bake in 325° oven 1 hour or until a knife inserted in center comes out clean. Cut in squares and serve with Mushroom-Pimiento Sauce. Makes 8 servings.

**Mushroom-Pimiento Sauce:** Combine 1 (10½ oz.) can condensed cream of mushroom soup and 1 c. dairy sour cream in small saucepan. Gradually stir in ¼ c. milk. Add ¼ c. chopped pimientos. Heat over low heat, stirring constantly.

## Mexican Sour Cream Enchiladas

*Turkey-stuffed enchiladas topped with sour cream*

| | |
|---|---|
| ½ c. chopped onion | 1½ tsp. chili powder |
| 1 (4 oz.) can mushrooms, | 1 tsp. ground cumin |
| drained | ½ tsp. salt |
| 1 clove garlic, minced | ¼ tsp. pepper |
| 2 tblsp. butter or | Cooking oil |
| regular margarine | 18 tortillas, canned |
| 1½ c. finely chopped | or frozen |
| cooked turkey | and thawed |
| 1 (4 oz.) can green | 4 c. shredded Cheddar |
| chilies, drained | cheese |
| and chopped | 2 c. dairy sour cream |
| 1 c. dairy sour cream | |

• Saute onion, mushrooms and garlic in melted

butter in 3-qt. saucepan until tender (do not brown). Add turkey, chilies, 1 c. sour cream, chili powder, cumin, salt and pepper. Heat over low heat, stirring frequently, until hot. Remove from heat.

• Meanwhile, pour oil into 8" skillet, filling about ½" deep. Fry tortillas in hot oil until soft (about 3 seconds). Drain on paper towels.

• Spread a heaping tablespoon of filling in center of each tortilla. Sprinkle with Cheddar cheese. Fold sides over filling. Place seam side down in greased 13×9×2" baking dish. Repeat filling and folding procedure with remaining tortillas.

• Bake in 350° oven 15 minutes. Spread with 2 c. sour cream and sprinkle with remaining Cheddar cheese. Bake 8 minutes more. (Watch time carefully so sour cream does not curdle.) Makes 6 servings.

## English Turkey Vegetable Pie

*Delicious country-style turkey and vegetable pie*

| | |
|---|---|
| Flaky English Pastry (recipe follows) | 1 c. water |
| 2 medium potatoes, pared and cubed | 1 tsp. salt |
| 2 large carrots, cubed | 2 c. cubed cooked turkey |
| 1 c. sliced celery | 1 (2 oz.) can mushrooms |
| ⅓ c. chopped onion | 1 (10½ oz.) can condensed cream of chicken soup |
| ½ c. fresh or frozen peas | ¼ c. chopped pimientos |

• Prepare Flaky English Pastry and chill in refrigerator 1 hour.

• Combine potatoes, carrots, celery, onion, peas, water and salt in 2-qt. saucepan. Bring mixture to a boil. Reduce heat; cover and simmer 10 minutes or until vegetables are tender. Drain.

• Add turkey, undrained mushrooms, chicken soup and pimientos. Heat well.

• Roll out ⅔ of pastry on floured surface to 14" circle. Place in 10" pie plate, adjusting to fit. Trim edges. Pour hot turkey mixture into pastry-lined pie plate.

• Roll out remaining pastry. Adjust top crust and flute edges; cut vents.

• Bake in 425° oven 35 minutes or until golden brown. Makes 6 servings.

**Flaky English Pastry:** Sift together 2 c. sifted flour, 2 tsp. baking powder and 1 tsp. salt into bowl. Cut in ⅔ c. shortening with pastry blender until mixture is crumbly. Combine 1 egg yolk, beaten, 1 tblsp. lemon juice and ½ c. hot water. Add to dry ingredients; toss just until moistened. Shape into a ball. Wrap in plastic wrap.

## Golden Turkey Lasagne

*An unusual turkey dish with an Italian accent*

| | |
|---|---|
| ½ c. chopped onion | ½ tsp. dried basil leaves |
| ½ c. chopped green pepper | 8 oz. lasagne noodles, cooked and drained |
| 3 tblsp. butter or regular margarine | 1½ c. cream-style cottage cheese |
| 1 (4 oz.) can mushrooms, drained | 3 c. cubed cooked turkey |
| ¼ c. chopped pimientos | 2 c. shredded Cheddar cheese |
| 1 (10½ oz.) can condensed cream of chicken soup | ½ c. grated Parmesan cheese |
| ⅓ c. milk | |

• Saute onion and green pepper in melted butter in 2-qt. saucepan until tender (do not brown). Stir in mushrooms, pimientos, soup, milk and basil. Heat well.

• Arrange ½ of the noodles in greased 13×9×2" baking dish. Then layer in ½ of the sauce, ½ of cottage cheese, ½ of the turkey, ½ of the Cheddar cheese and ½ of the Parmesan cheese. Repeat layers, ending with Parmesan cheese.

• Bake in 350° oven 45 minutes or until hot and bubbly. Makes 6 to 8 servings.

## Turkey Corn Chowder

*This hearty chowder is great on a cold winter day*

| | |
|---|---|
| 8 strips bacon | 4 c. cubed cooked turkey |
| 2 c. chopped onion | 1 (17 oz.) can whole kernel corn |
| 4 c. sliced, pared potatoes | 1 (17 oz.) can cream-style corn |
| 1 (10¾ oz.) can condensed chicken broth | 2 c. light cream |
| ½ tsp. salt | ¼ tsp. pepper |
| | Chopped fresh parsley |

• Cook bacon in 4-qt. saucepan or Dutch oven until crisp. Remove and drain on paper towels. Crumble bacon. Set aside.

• Pour off drippings; reserve ¼ c. Saute onion in ¼ c. drippings until tender (do not brown).

• Add potatoes, chicken broth and salt. Bring mixture to a boil. Reduce heat; cover and simmer 10 minutes or until potatoes are tender. Add turkey, undrained corn, cream-style corn, light cream and pepper. Heat well.

**To serve:** Garnish each bowl of soup with bacon bits and parsley. Serve with assorted crackers. Makes about 3 quarts or 9 servings.

# The wonderful smell

When does the Christmas season begin at your house? In the past, the holiday season in many homes began the week after Thanksgiving when grandmother would invite all the grandchildren to come and help her bake fruitcake and nut bread.

For several days, the kitchen was adrift with the rich spicy smells: mincemeat bubbled in a huge kettle, and paper-thin ginger cookies were cooling on racks alongside rich fruitcakes laden with raisins and nuts. If this brings back childhood memories of good things baking for Christmas and awakens a certain yearning to share those experiences with your family, then gather everyone together to bake and decorate our beautiful cakes and breads. Many are easy enough for youngsters to decorate while some require the skilled adult touch.

There's something to please everyone: Men will especially like the Sugarplum Coffee Ring—the children will be delighted with the jaunty Merry Santa Cake. A Christmastime birthday child will feel extra special when you bring out the Peppermint Cream Sponge all aglow with red candles. Surprise the family on Christmas morning and serve the Cinnamon-Walnut Twist for a breakfast treat. Instead of serving the usual pumpkin or mince pie for Christmas day dinner, present the Glazed Fruit Gateau on your most handsome crystal plate. It's truly an elegant dessert—and though it looks like a French masterpiece that took hours to make, it really is quite simple to prepare. If you are searching for an unusual gift to give to someone special, bake an extra gateau. Wrapped in foil and tied with a huge red bow, this cake would be a beautiful homemade holiday gift.

Many of these festive breads and cakes can be made a month ahead and frozen. After Thanksgiving why not plan to fill your kitchen with the sweet smells of Christmas!

When friends and neighbors drop in to say "Merry Christmas," invite them to stay for coffee and homemade cake or bread. You will be proud to serve any one of these gorgeous holiday creations—all are home-baked and hand-decorated. Clockwise: Glazed Fruit Gateau, Cinnamon-Walnut Twist, Christmas Star Coffee Cake, Sugarplum Coffee Ring and Glorious Golden Fruitcake.

Photography/Richard Tomlinson

# of Christmas baking

## Christmas Motif Cake

*Looks so elegant. . . yet is easy to decorate*

| | |
|---|---|
| 2 (9″) round cake layers | Green food color |
| Lemon Butter Cream (recipe follows) | Red glossy decorating gel |

• Place 1 cake layer on serving plate.
• Tint 2 cups Lemon Butter Cream bright green. Spread on top of cake layer. Top with remaining cake layer. Frost sides and top of cake.
• Cut a Christmas motif from a discarded Christmas greeting card, such as: angel, snowman, small child, Nativity scene or Santa. Cut a piece of aluminum foil the same size. Place motif on foil and put in center of cake.
• Using tip 96 with white Lemon Butter Cream, pipe small flowers around edge of Christmas motif.
• Using red glossy decorating gel, pipe centers in each small flower.
• Press a star- or bell-shaped cookie cutter into sides of cake in 5 places. Fill impression made by cutter with small white flowers using tip 96.
• Using tip 21 with remaining white Lemon Butter Cream, pipe a border around top edge of cake. Makes 12 servings.

**Lemon Butter Cream:** Mix together ¾ c. shortening and ¼ c. soft butter or regular margarine. Gradually add 1 (1 lb.) box confectioners sugar alternately with 5 tsp. milk, beating well after each addition. Beat in ¾ tsp. salt and 2 tsp. lemon extract.

## Red and Green Holiday Bells

*Ring in the New Year with these bright holiday bells*

| | |
|---|---|
| 1 (18½ oz.) pkg. yellow cake mix | Green food color |
| | Red food color |
| Decorating Frosting (recipe follows) | Red glossy decorating gel |

• Prepare yellow cake mix according to package directions. Pour batter into 2 greased and floured foil bell-shaped cake pans. (Can be purchased in either variety stores or supermarkets.) Bake according to package directions for layer cake pans.
• Arrange bells side by side on large serving tray. Frost sides and top of bells with 2½ c. white Decorating Frosting. (Reserve some for center of flowers.)
• Tint 1 cup Decorating Frosting bright green. (Reserve some for leaves.) Using tip 96, pipe small flower border along bottom edge of bells. Then pipe flower border along top edge.
• Using tip 3 with white Decorating Frosting, pipe small white centers in each flower in the borders.
• Tint 1½ c. Decorating Frosting red. Using tip 97, make 6 large red roses. Place 3 roses near top of each bell. Make several small buds and place in an attractive design.
• Using tip 99 and remaining green Decorating Frosting, pipe leaves among roses where needed.
• Using red glossy decorating gel, pipe *Happy New Year* across both bells. Makes 16 to 20 servings.

**Decorating Frosting:** Combine 2 (1 lb.) boxes confectioners sugar and 1 tsp. cream of tartar in large bowl. Add 6 egg whites and 1 tsp. almond extract. Beat with electric mixer at low speed until well mixed. Then beat at high speed, scraping bowl occasionally, until mixture is stiff and holds its shape. Keep frosting covered with wet paper towels so it will not dry out. Divide frosting as follows: 2½ c. untinted and 2½ c. to be tinted.

## Sugarplum Coffee Ring

*This tasty coffee cake decorates itself while baking*

| | |
|---|---|
| ½ c. milk | 1¼ tsp. ground cinnamon |
| ⅓ c. shortening | 6 tblsp. melted butter or regular margarine |
| ⅓ c. sugar | |
| 1 tsp. salt | ½ c. toasted slivered almonds |
| 1 pkg. active dry yeast | |
| ¼ c. lukewarm water | ½ c. quartered red candied cherries |
| 2 eggs | |
| 3¼ c. sifted flour | ⅓ c. dark corn syrup |
| 1 c. sugar | |

• Scald milk in saucepan. Add to shortening, ⅓ c. sugar and salt in bowl. Cool to lukewarm.
• Sprinkle yeast on lukewarm water; stir to dissolve. Add yeast, eggs and 1 c. flour to milk mixture. Beat with electric mixer at medium speed until smooth, about 2 minutes, scraping bowl occasionally. Or beat with spoon until batter is smooth.
• Gradually add enough flour to make a soft dough that leaves the sides of the bowl. Place dough in lightly greased bowl; turn over to grease top. Cover and let rise in warm place until doubled, about 2 hours.
• Punch down dough. Let rest 10 minutes.
• Turn dough out on lightly floured surface. Divide dough in thirds. Cut each third into 12 parts. Shape into balls.

• Combine 1 c. sugar and cinnamon. Dip balls in melted butter and then in sugar-cinnamon mixture. (Reserve remaining melted butter for drizzle.) Arrange 12 balls in greased 10″ tube pan with solid bottom. (If your tube pan has a removable bottom, cover outside of pan with foil to prevent leakage.) Sprinkle with almonds and cherries. Repeat layers twice more.

• Mix together corn syrup and remaining melted butter from dipping balls. Drizzle on top. Cover and let rise until doubled, about 1 hour.

• Bake in 350° oven 35 minutes or until done. Cool in pan on rack 5 minutes. Remove from pan. Serve slightly warm, top-side up on serving plate. Makes 10 to 12 servings.

## Glazed Fruit Gateau

*Truly a work of art—so easy to make*

| | |
|---|---|
| 2 (9″) round sponge or yellow cake layers | 14 maraschino cherries, drained |
| 1 (3¼ oz.) pkg. lemon pudding and pie filling | ¾ c. peach or apricot preserves |
| 1½ tsp. grated lemon rind | 1 c. heavy cream |
| 1 (1 lb. 13 oz.) can pear halves, drained | 1 tblsp. sugar |
| | 1 tsp. vanilla |
| 1 (8¾ oz.) can apricot halves, drained | 1 drop yellow food color |
| | ½ c. toasted sliced almonds |

• Cut cake in half horizontally, making 4 layers.

• Prepare lemon pudding and pie filling according to package directions. Remove from heat. Stir in lemon rind. Cool well.

• Reserve 4 pear halves, 5 apricot halves and 4 maraschino cherries; set aside. Chop remaining fruit. Fold into filling.

• Spread lemon filling between cake layers. Arrange reserved pears and apricots in a symmetrical design, cut side down on top layer. Cut reserved maraschino cherries in half. Place on each side of pears.

• Melt peach preserves in small saucepan over low heat. Press through a sieve. Quickly spoon or brush mixture over fruit.

• Whip heavy cream until thickened. Add sugar, vanilla and food color. Beat until soft peaks form. Reserve ½ c.; set aside. Swirl remaining cream on sides of cake.

• Stud sides of cake with almonds.

• Using tip 21 (large rosette) and reserved cream, pipe a border around top edge of cake. Refrigerate until serving time. Makes 12 servings.

## Merry Santa Cake

*Sure to delight any young child*

| | |
|---|---|
| 1 (18½ oz.) pkg. yellow cake mix | 2 small black gumdrops |
| Peppermint Butter Cream (recipe follows) | 1 black licorice string |
| | 1 large red gumdrop |
| Flaked coconut | Red colored sugar |
| Red glossy decorating gel | |

• Prepare yellow cake mix according to package directions. Pour batter into 2 greased and floured foil Santa-shaped cake pans. (Can be purchased in either variety stores or supermarkets.) Bake according to package directions for layer cake pans.

• Place 1 Santa layer on serving plate. (Freeze other one for later use. Or, to decorate both at once, double the decorating ingredients listed above.)

• Frost sides and top of cake with Peppermint Butter Cream.

• Arrange coconut over beard and mustache area. Use red glossy decorating gel to fill in hat area. Place black gumdrops in position for eyes. Cut black licorice string into short pieces and place in position for eyebrows. Cut large red gumdrop into pieces for both the nose and the mouth. Place on face. Sprinkle red colored sugar on cheeks.

• Using tip 21 with remaining white Peppermint Butter Cream, pipe two or three wavy lines along bottom edge of hat. Also accent tassel with a large puff of frosting. Each cake serves 8.

**Peppermint Butter Cream:** Combine 1 (1 lb.) box confectioners sugar, ½ c. soft shortening, 2 tblsp. soft butter or regular margarine and ½ tsp. salt in bowl. Beat with electric mixer at low speed until well mixed. Gradually add ⅓ c. milk, 1½ tsp. vanilla and ½ tsp. peppermint extract; beat until smooth.

## Glorious Golden Fruitcake

*Drizzle with creamy white glaze, and top with pecans*

| | |
|---|---|
| 4 c. sifted flour | 1 c. golden raisins |
| 1½ tsp. baking powder | ½ c. chopped red candied cherries |
| ½ tsp. salt | |
| 2 c. butter or regular margarine | ½ c. chopped green candied cherries |
| 2½ c. sugar | 1 tblsp. grated lemon rind |
| 6 eggs | |
| ¼ c. milk | Pineapple Glaze (recipe follows) |
| 4 c. chopped walnuts | |
| ½ c. chopped candied pineapple | Pecan halves |

• Sift together flour, baking powder and salt.

Reserve ¼ c.; set aside.

• Cream together butter and sugar until light and fluffy. Add eggs, one at a time, beating well after each addition. Add sifted dry ingredients alternately with milk, beating well after each addition.

• Combine walnuts, pineapple, raisins, candied cherries, lemon rind and reserved ¼ c. flour; toss gently to coat. Stir into batter. Spread batter in greased and waxed paper-lined 10″ tube pan.

• Bake in 275° oven 2 hours 45 minutes or until cake tests done. Cool in pan on rack 30 minutes. Remove from pan; cool on rack.

• Wrap fruitcake tightly in foil. Store in refrigerator up to 4 weeks. (Fruitcake keeps better if stored unfrosted.)

**To serve:** Prepare Pineapple Glaze. Frost top of cake, letting glaze drip down sides. Decorate cake with pecan halves. Makes 1 (5 lb.) fruitcake.

**Pineapple Glaze:** Combine 1 c. sifted confectioners sugar and 2 tblsp. pineapple juice; mix until smooth.

## Peppermint Cream Sponge

*Peppermint cream topping adds a festive touch*

| | |
|---|---|
| 1¼ c. sifted flour | 3 (2 oz.) env. whipped |
| 1 c. sugar | topping mix |
| ½ tsp. baking powder | ¾ c. crushed pepper- |
| ½ tsp. salt | mint candies |
| 6 eggs, separated | 3 drops red food color |
| 1 tsp. cream of tartar | 12 red and white |
| ½ c. sugar | peppermint candy |
| ¼ c. water | rounds |
| 1 tsp. vanilla | Silver dragees |
| 1½ c. milk | 12 cinnamon red hots |

• Sift together flour, 1 c. sugar, baking powder and salt.

• Beat egg whites in bowl at high speed until frothy. Add cream of tartar. Gradually add ½ c. sugar, beating until stiff, but not dry, peaks form.

• Combine egg yolks, water, vanilla and dry ingredients in small bowl. Beat at medium high speed until thick and lemon colored (about 4 minutes).

• Gradually fold egg yolk mixture into egg whites. Pour batter into ungreased 10″ tube pan.

• Bake in 350° oven 45 minutes or until cake tests done. Invert tube pan on funnel or bottle to cool. When completely cooled, remove from pan.

• Combine milk and whipped topping mix in bowl. Prepare according to package directions. Fold in

crushed peppermint and red food color. Refrigerate until needed.

• Place cake upside down. Slice off entire top of cake 1″ down and set aside. Make cuts down into cake 1″ from outer edge of hole. With spoon, remove cake within cuts, being careful to leave a base of cake 1″ thick. Place cake on plate.

• Fill hollow with whipped topping. Place top of cake in position. Frost sides and top of cake with remaining whipped topping.

• Place round peppermint candies at even intervals around sides of cake about 1″ from bottom. Form arches over the peppermint candies with silver dragees. (Hint: Use tweezers to position silver dragees.) At bottom of each arch, place a cinnamon red hot. Refrigerate until serving time. Makes 12 servings.

## Cinnamon-Walnut Twist

*These stollens are perfect holiday hostess gifts*

| | |
|---|---|
| ¾ c. milk | ½ c. raisins |
| 1 c. butter or regular | 1 c. brown sugar, |
| margarine | firmly packed |
| ⅓ c. sugar | 1 c. chopped walnuts |
| ½ tsp. salt | 1 tsp. ground cinnamon |
| 1 pkg. active dry yeast | ⅓ c. melted butter or |
| 2 tblsp. sugar | regular margarine |
| ¼ c. lukewarm water | Vanilla Icing (recipe |
| 4½ c. sifted flour | follows) |
| 2 eggs | Red candied cherries |
| ½ tsp. grated lemon rind | Pecan halves |
| ½ c. mixed candied fruit | |

• Scald milk in saucepan. Add to 1 c. butter, ⅓ c. sugar and salt in bowl. Cool to lukewarm.

• Sprinkle yeast and 2 tblsp. sugar on lukewarm water; stir to dissolve. Add yeast and 1 c. flour to milk mixture. Beat with electric mixer at medium speed until smooth, about 2 minutes, scraping bowl occasionally.

• Add eggs and lemon rind; beat well. Stir in candied fruit and raisins. Gradually add enough flour to make a soft dough that leaves the sides of the bowl. Turn onto lightly floured surface; knead until smooth and satiny, about 8 to 10 minutes.

• Place in lightly greased bowl; turn dough over to grease top. Cover and let rise in warm place until doubled, about 2 hours.

• Combine brown sugar, walnuts and cinnamon; mix well. Set aside.

• Divide dough in half. Roll each half into 12×10″

rectangle. Brush with half of ⅓ c. melted butter. Sprinkle with half of cinnamon-walnut mixture. Fold dough in thirds lengthwise by folding from one side to center and then fold opposite side over, making three layers. Place on greased baking sheet. Cut a slit through the center to within 2″ of each end. Fold one end over and out of slit. Fold other end under and out of slit. (This gives coffee cake a twisted look.) Cover and let rise until doubled, about 45 minutes.

• Bake in 375° oven 25 to 30 minutes or until done. While warm, spread with Vanilla Icing. Decorate stollens with red candied cherries and pecan halves. Makes 2 stollens.

**Vanilla Icing:** Combine 1½ c. sifted confectioners sugar, 3 tblsp. milk and 1 tsp. vanilla in bowl; mix until icing is smooth.

## Christmas Star Coffee Cake

*Bright red poinsettias accent the points*

| | |
|---|---|
| 1 c. milk | 1½ c. chopped red |
| ⅓ c. butter or regular | candied cherries |
| margarine | 1 c. honey |
| ½ c. sugar | Melted butter or |
| 1 tsp. salt | regular margarine |
| ½ tsp. ground cardamom | Vanilla Frosting (recipe |
| 2 pkgs. active dry yeast | follows) |
| ¼ c. lukewarm water | Red and green candied |
| 4½ c. sifted flour | cherries |
| 1 egg | Pecan halves |
| 3 c. chopped pecans | |

• Scald milk. Add to ⅓ c. butter, ½ c. sugar, salt and cardamom in bowl. Cool to lukewarm.

• Sprinkle yeast on lukewarm water; stir to dissolve. Add yeast and 1 c. flour to milk mixture. Beat with electric mixer at medium speed until smooth, about 2 minutes, scraping bowl occasionally. Or beat with spoon until batter is smooth.

• Add egg; beat well. Gradually add enough flour to make a soft dough that leaves the sides of the bowl. Turn onto lightly floured surface; knead until smooth and satiny, about 8 to 10 minutes.

• Place in lightly greased bowl; turn dough over to grease top. Cover and let rise in warm place until doubled, about 1½ hours. Punch down dough. Let rest 10 minutes.

• Combine pecans, candied cherries and honey; mix well. Divide in half; set aside. (Use half of cherry-nut filling in each coffee cake.)

• Turn dough out on floured surface. Divide dough in half. Roll each half into 14″ circle. Place on greased baking sheet. Cut 6 (3″) slits about 7½″ apart in circle, forming 6 triangles. Brush dough

with melted butter.

• Spread 1 heaping tablespoon of filling in each triangle about ½″ from outside edge. Fold one corner of triangle over filling. Then fold other corner over, forming point of star. Repeat folding procedure making a 6-pointed star. Spread remaining filling in center of star. Cover and let rise until doubled, about 30 minutes.

• Bake in 350° oven 25 minutes or until done. Remove from baking sheets; cool on racks.

• Frost points of star coffee cakes with Vanilla Frosting. Decorate alternate points with poinsettias made by cutting petals from red candied cherries and stems and leaves from green candied cherries. Place pecan halves on remaining points. Makes 2 coffee cakes.

**Vanilla Frosting:** Combine 2½ c. sifted confectioners sugar, 2 tblsp. soft butter or regular margarine, 3 tblsp. milk and 1 tsp. vanilla; beat until smooth.

## Golden Miniature Fruitcakes

*Freeze these ahead for holiday gift-giving*

| | |
|---|---|
| 4 c. sifted flour | 4 c. cut-up candied |
| 2 tsp. baking powder | pineapple |
| 2 tsp. ground cinnamon | 3 c. chopped pecans |
| 1½ tsp. ground nutmeg | 1½ c. halved red |
| ½ tsp. salt | candied cherries |
| 2 c. butter or regular | 1 tblsp. grated lemon |
| margarine | rind |
| 2 c. brown sugar, firmly | Icing (recipe follows) |
| packed | Mixed candied fruit |
| 12 eggs | |

• Sift together flour, baking powder, cinnamon, nutmeg and salt. Reserve ⅓ c.; set aside.

• Cream together butter and brown sugar until light and fluffy. Add eggs, one at a time, beating well after each addition. Gradually add flour mixture; mix well.

• Combine reserved ⅓ c. flour, pineapple, pecans, cherries and lemon rind. Stir into batter. Spoon batter into 12 greased and floured 10½ oz. soup cans, filling 1″ from the top.

• Bake in 275° oven 1 hour 15 minutes or until cakes test done. Remove from cans; cool on racks.

• Lay fruitcakes on side and frost with Icing, letting some drip down sides. Decorate with candied fruit cut in flowers and leaves. Makes 12.

**Icing:** Combine 2 c. sifted confectioners sugar, 1 tblsp. soft butter or regular margarine, 1 tblsp. milk and ½ tsp. vanilla. Stir until smooth.

# Christmas

We climbed the straight tamarack
In those days,
Clinging fast to limb and limb,
Inspecting branches for strong footholds,
Leaning out to reach the little cones,
To discover the best ones were
Really at the top
Where the wind pushed and pulled the spire point,
The red-winged blackbird's perch,
Now grown cold and vacant
In winter's air.
The needles dropped away
From the deciduous conifer
To leave the twigs all bare,
A brittle silhouette above the humps of swamp,
And little saucers of blue ice.
Our footprints to the tree
In the snow looked small and gray,
Frozen writings of mute reality,
Our sudden past. We would trace them
Home again, our pockets full of cones
For school children to paint
And weave with yarn into chains
To hang upon another tree.

—Claire Mattern

# Let Nature be your holiday decorator

The power of Christmas, the "festival of light and fire," lies in its blend of spiritual and earthly beauty. For sheer sensuousness and warmth, it has no equal among holidays. For centuries, we have indulged to the fullest our love of decoration, adorning our houses and decking our halls.

But in recent decades, certainly in the United States, the tendency has inclined more and more toward the artificial. To earlier eyes, the artificial must have been astonishing—imagine the first fragile Christmas ball, so delicate that it could shatter at a harsh touch, and the first shimmering string of electric lights. . . they were magical. But at that time, we took for granted the good things of our good earth. And today, when it is the things of the earth that are becoming rare and precious, and the purchased and artificial that are taken for granted, the glitter of tinsel and plastic loses its appeal.

This year return to the good earth theme with your children and make a delightful assortment of Christmas decorations from Nature's collectibles.

Part of the charm of making decorations like the ones we give instructions for on the following pages is that you can indulge your instinct for collecting. Another appealing quality is that they are all made with your own hands. The charm of handmade Christmas decorations harkens back to an earlier time, but is still as satisfying today—perhaps even more so now, when making things is a revived pleasure for so many. In the old-fashioned Christmas as Paul Engle said, ". . . our hands seemed to create so much more of it then than now. . . . The entire family either sewed, whittled, knit, sawed, nailed, crocheted, embroidered, baked, pasted, or cracked to celebrate that generous day. . . ."

**What to gather ahead**

Natural things are there for the taking, both at Christmastime and during the earlier autumn months. Early fall and winter is a fine bright time to begin collecting materials from fields, woods, garden and shore to enhance your Christmas home.

Keep in mind the different uses to which materials can be put—wreaths and sprays; ornaments to hang on the tree; espaliered trees and little table trees; circles of greens to surround candles or lamps; decorated Yule logs; doorway decorations, table centerpieces and sideboard pieces; garlands and festoons to hang over mantels, windows and doorways, or draped along banisters. Separate arrangements of leaves, cones and pods, or special creations like the pine cone stocking are all good ideas to keep in mind as you begin to search the countryside for the following things, which can be used as they are or preserved.

**Materials to use as they are:** pine cones, nuts, acorns, burrs, berries, flower calyxes, shells, seed pods, twigs, bark, branches.

**Materials to be dried or preserved:** berries, pods, garden flowers, Queen Anne's lace, goldenrod, Joe-Pye weed, mosses, leaves, grasses, fronds, dock, teasel, corn husks, straw.

There are several methods for drying flowers and/or pods. You can simply hang the collected material in an airy place until thoroughly dried (pods should be left on the stalk to dry), or they can be preserved in a glycerine solution. Leaves that lend themselves well to a glycerine treatment are broad-leaf evergreens, galax and magnolia. Instructions for specific leaves vary, but the general procedure in using glycerine, which can be purchased in any drug store, is to mix one part glycerine to one or two parts water and stand the stems in the solution for one to three weeks until they are shiny and have taken on a bronze hue.

There are so many different kinds of seed pods that lend themselves to Christmas ornaments that it is worth mentioning a few specifically: Chinese lantern, ground cherry, poppy, iris, yucca, okra, morning glory, hosta, eucalyptus, milkweed and love-in-a-mist.

The berries gathered well before Christmas can be dried. But late-blooming berries can be preserved until Christmas by spraying them right after picking with an anti-desiccant, such as Wilt-Proof or Foli-Gard, available in garden stores. Another prolonging procedure is to add fertilizer to the water in which the branches are standing. Any water-soluble fertilizer will do, Peters' products being among the best. Bayberry, barberry, pyracanthus, bittersweet, Chinese tallow berries (also called "popcorn" in some parts of the country) are good berries to choose.

### Supplies to gather

To make ornaments and other decorations you might want to have some or all of these supplies on hand: wires (various weights), florists' wire, shellac, clear acrylic spray, glue, spray paints, silica gel, wire mesh, chicken wire, yarn, plywood, Styrofoam, ribbon, sharp shears.

### What to gather at Christmastime

There are many natural materials widely available at Christmastime because they are traditionally used in the American Christmas. Evergreens, of course—spruce, hemlock, balsam fir, juniper, yew, arborvitae and pine among others. Other plants which are evergreen are box, ivy, privet, laurel and holly—holly and ivy being two of the most venerable Christmas greens. Materials less frequently used, but still widely available, include fruits—apples, lady apples, lemons, limes, oranges, kumquats, small bananas and cranberries—and a vegetable—bright red peppers, which can be used with striking effect in many wreaths and arrangements.

### A smattering of suggestions

There are many more ways to use natural materials for Christmas decorations than those we show here. Don't hesitate to let your imagination lead you. Sometimes techniques are the only barrier between your own creativity and a show-stopping success. So here are some tips:

• Wreaths and festoons can be made on wire or rope, or around a bent coat hanger. Della Robbia wreaths, inspired by the terra-cotta wreaths made by the della Robbia family in 15th century Italy, can be constructed to hang on doors—with the greens, fruits and cones wired together. Or use Della-Robbia-like circles as centerpieces, on a sideboard, or surrounding a punch bowl, hurricane lamp or candles. For centerpieces the fruit can be scattered rather than wired.

• Beautiful wreaths can also be made with English ivy, nuts, berries, dried or fresh flowers, treated with glycerine leaves. Holly and boxwood also lend themselves naturally to wreaths.

• Kissing balls—a favorite Christmas decoration hung from doorways or hallway light fixtures—can be made with cones, pods, all of the greens mentioned earlier and dried berries. Using a large Styrofoam ball as the base, wrap materials with florists' wire and then insert them into the Styrofoam until the ball is completely covered. Accents of gingham or plaid ribbons can add an old-fashioned touch of color.

• Boxwood and other greens can be beautiful if sprayed gold, silver or flat white. Try an arrangement of leaves and cones sprayed dull white, with a few carnations for brilliance. Apples and other fruits lend themselves well to gilding (golden apples were a traditional decoration in the early days of our country). And large leaves can be painted for a totally different look as were the red rhododendron leaves circled with glitter (see picture).

• Pine cones can be cut crosswise to form flower-like hangings or fashioned into owl shapes. Milkweed pods lend themselves especially well to Christmas ornamentation and can be combined to create beautiful flowers (see pictures).

• Fruits can be piled among greens or piled into pyramids with sprigs of green. Apples alone can form a striking pyramid—or lemons and limes. Fruits can be sprayed or painted with lacquer, which not only gives them brilliance but will also help preserve them. Berries also may be gilded or sprayed with lacquer (excepting bayberries, which lose their luster). At average temperatures, berries should last through the holidays.

• Nuts can be painted too, or in a tradition that goes back a very long time, they can be wrapped in gold or silver foil or in colored paper to be used as Christmas tree ornaments. Nuts can be wired into grape-like clusters or made into small trees like the pearlized nut tree shown. (To use nuts, pierce them with a drill or a red-hot pin and insert wire.)

To some eyes, however, nuts, berries, pods, dried leaves and flowers may be at their most beautiful when used completely naturally—sans silver, gold or paint. Then they are more reminiscent of the bright day when they were collected from woods or field. But, collected on a morning or afternoon in the summer or early fall, all natural ornaments will have a second existence, recollected in the tranquility of winter's snow, by the warmth of a Christmas fire, in the embrace of another tree.

Photography/Fred Carbone    Design/Mrs. Charles E. Barnes, Jr., Drexel Hill, Pa. (Spruce Hill Garden Club)

This Fairyland Tree uses natural materials only—baby's breath, Queen Anne's lace, rhododendron leaves, milkweed fluff.
• Spray Queen Anne's lace (which has been pre-dried in silica gel) and baby's breath with white paint. When dry, place at random on tree branches.
• Coat 1½'' to 3'' Styrofoam balls with white glue; shake in bag filled with milkweed fluff. Insert paper-clip hooks or wire; reinforce them with glue.
• Roll rhododendron leaves into cornucopias, wrap with facial tissue, secure with wire twist. Insert cornucopias made from 4 thicknesses of newspaper into each rhododendron leaf, stuff with paper to hold outside surface smooth.
• Place in 100° oven to dry; it takes about four days. Remove facial tissue, spray outside with coat of white, then 2 coats of red (let dry between coats). Remove stuffing, spray insides the same way.
• For tree-topper, spray a bouquet of foxtail grass with aluminum paint.

Design/Mrs. Walter Hutcheson, West Chester, Pa. (West Chester Planters)

Photography/Bob Robinson

Photography/Jean Gillies

To make stocking (above), use #20 and #22 wire (heavier gauge for larger cones). Wire cones in groups of three to five, attach to wire mesh. Drill holes in chestnuts, walnuts and acorns; insert wire and attach to mesh backing. Spray with clear acrylic; back with felt.

For door arrangements using natural materials, wire lemons, apples, cones, greens and ribbons to wire mesh backing shaped to your specifications.

Design/Mrs. Wilson B. Harkins, Jr., Lansdowne, Pa. (Martha Washington Garden Club)     Photo Stylist/Rachel Martens

Create the warm glow of Christmas in your home with a festoon of sweetgum and milkweed pod flowers and a festive pearl-nut tree centerpiece.

To make the milkweed pod flowers, first clean the pods, then glue 3″ pieces of pipe cleaners to blunt end of each pod; dry overnight. Gather five pods, wrap pipe cleaner ends with florist's wire to form a flower. Glue an acorn cap into the center; glue pine cone petals around it.

To make pearl-nut tree, start with a 12″ Styrofoam cone. Wrap about 2 pounds of assorted nuts with nylon pieces cut from an old stocking. Pull nylon tight, hold ends in place with florist's wire. Attach wrapped nuts to cone wth hair pins, starting at the bottom. Spray tree with silver (be sure to use paints recommended for Styrofoam). When dry, spray with several coats of white (dry between coats). Finish with one or two coats of pearl spray paint.

Design/Mrs. Clark R. Morris, Drexel Hill, Pa. (Drexelbrook Garden Club)

A Madonna made of natural materials is sure to be admired. To make the cardboard-backed Madonna (above), arrange dried natural materials to form the figure. This one uses allium albo-pilosum, allium tomentum, berginia, viburnum sieboldi, cherry laurel, eleagnus pungens, lavender, fern fronds, Japanese cut-leaf maple and a milkweed pod. Highlight some of the pieces with gold or silver spray; when dry, glue figure to cardboard.

To make the ivy Madonna (right), cut plywood to shape and size—this one is 3' high. Glue bird seed to face, hands and feet, using dark seeds for the eye. Staple yucca in position for wings. Staple large ivy leaves (leaf tops pointing down) in position for skirt, small leaves (pointing upward) for bodice. Make cap from small ivy leaves; add cornhusk curls.

All kinds of whimsical tree ornaments can be fashioned from natural materials collected in summer and fall.

One-of-a-kind ornaments (top photos) result from imaginative combinations of cones, milkweed fluff, seed pods, gourds, holly berries and milkweed pod flowers.

A candle-bearing caroler and the tree figures (left) came out of the creative minds of Shipley School children. Leaves and cornhusks shaped around twigs form the body of the nut-headed, feather-topped figure. Nuts, pods and corn turned into boy, bird, nest and worm perched on a tree-like branch.

Design/Shipley School Art Dept., Bryn Mawr, Pa.

# Handcrafted nativity scenes

## Nature provides the materials

Materials for creating your own nativity scene are free for the collecting—from the backyard, fields, roadside or river bank. The result of your efforts will be a cherished family reminder of that first Christmas 2000 years ago.

The charming figures we show are modeled by Clara Nell Howell—from clay she finds near their farm in Alabama. "Dig for clay a few feet below the natural surface of the soil along creek or ditch banks," she suggests. Also, "remember to hollow out the figures from the bottom if you fire them in a kiln." (Children often prefer to work with self-hardening clay—from art or hobby shops.) She models the crèche figures in a size and shape to fit the "nature finds" used for the setting.

These handcrafted nativity scenes can involve the whole family. You may start a family tradition that will be handed down for generations.

A gnarled branch provides an inviting resting place for Mary on the journey home from Bethlehem (above). She was modeled in a sitting position to fit the branch. Joseph is only 4½ inches tall. The donkey grazes nearby, on dried lawn clippings.

Knobby gourd becomes a tree ornament when you saw off the front to
make a window for creche figures. They're really tiny—only 1 ½ inches.
Children are especially adept at modeling these simple figures.

# Holiday decorations

Dried fungus forms a halo-like background for the manger scene (left). The smooth ivory color sets off the red clay figures. Mary and Joseph are a tiny 2½ inches tall; miniature sheep, 1 inch.

Flat 6- by 8-inch rock picked up on a hiking trip provides a platform for the Holy Family (below).

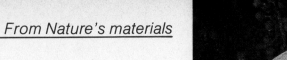

Gourd shell section provides shelter for the Christ Child and angel watching over Him (right). Bittersweet berries in background give you an idea of how petite the creche figures are.

Mesa-shaped pine knot (only 2 inches high) supports an angel hovering over the Holy Family (below). Mary sits on a stool modeled from clay.

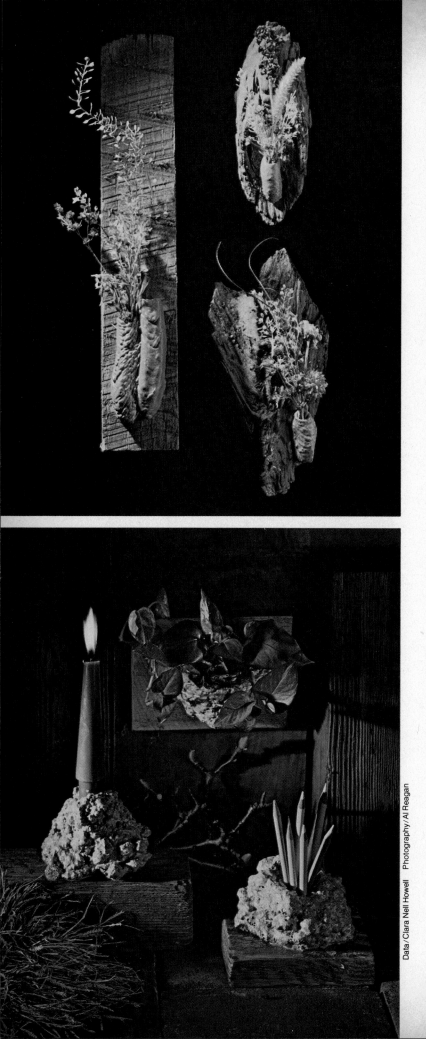

# Nature's pottery nests

**S**ometimes nature not only provides the clay, but supplies the potters as well. Mud-daubers and barn swallows are experts at knowing where to find the clay and how to build the most durable nests with it. When fired and glazed, these nests can turn into gifts that are most unusual as well as useful. Crayfish build interesting "chimneys" from clay.

Collect these clay creations *after* the nests have been abandoned. You'll find them under the eaves, on barn rafters or even on top of the ground when you're hiking through a meadow. Fire them in a kiln (cone 05) and glaze them both inside and out for greater durability (cone 06). Local ceramic or hobby shops will fire them for a nominal fee. Sometimes creature-potters do not use the best grade of clay and their work crumbles when fired. But in most cases, the pottery is well worth preserving.

The female mud-dauber seems to know by instinct where to find the best quality clay and spends most of her life constructing tubular cells for her babies. The number of cells varies from nest to nest. When you mount the fired and glazed tubes on pieces of weathered wood, you have stunning weed-holders (top photo).

Barn swallows are likely to use clay that's not too far away—often from the nearest mud puddle. So it may not always be of good enough quality to stand the firing. But if you were lucky enough to find a nest that survives the kiln, attach it to a board with waterproof cement, line it with foil and add soil and a philodendron for an eye-catching wall planter (lower left).

Since the crayfish lives deep in the earth, he has good sources of clay available to him. He's seldom seen since he works mostly at night building his chimney. Crayfish chimneys are found most often in low places and in limey soil. After you fire and glaze the chimney, you have a candleholder—or a pencil caddy for Dad's desk (shown at left).

Data/Clara Nell Howell   Photography/Al Reagan

# Ceramics without a kiln

**I**f you've always thought ceramics were beyond the realm of your can-do crafts, here's an easy way to add them to your skills. You don't need to buy a potter's wheel or an expensive kiln to make lasting objects of clay. In fact, all the items shown on these pages were made with just a rolling pin, sharp knife, paints and a glaze.

The good news comes in a package—Boneware Clay, which dries and hardens by contact with the air. It costs less than $3 for a 5-pound box. (If you have trouble finding it at your art or craft supply shop, write to Sculpture House, 38 East 30th Street, New York, N. Y. 10016 for a free catalog.)

Boneware Clay is easy to work with, simple enough for children from about age 10 and up to handle. Yet, it's creatively satisfying enough to hold the attention of adults. With no real training, you can turn out attractive and useful pieces on your first try. Imagine making your own buttons for a new spring coat or suit!

Photography/Fred Carbone    Design/Elizabeth Eaby

# Handmade gifts & decorations

For gifts that are different, try a landscape in clay. You can get raised effects—for trees or bushes or fences—by molding the clay with your fingers. For added depth, roll up clay in thin rounded strips; curl or curve them according to the design you're after, and press them onto the flat clay with your fingers.

You'll enjoy the feeling of craftsmanship that comes through working with clay. Your own imagination will lead you on to other shapes and objects than those shown here. All you have to do is learn these simple basic instructions—then you're on your own:

• To make flat objects, roll out clay on a wooden surface—a table top or old piece of wood will do—using rolling pin. Moisten clay with a sponge and smooth the surface with fingers until all lumps disappear.

• When the clay is flattened to about ¼-inch thickness, cut out the shapes you want to work with, using a sharp knife or an X-acto knife. Use the tip of the knife to inscribe your design into the clay surface, pressing very lightly. If you want a higher center (as in buttons), mold the clay gently with your fingers—working from the center to the edge. Don't forget to punch holes in Christmas tree ornaments and other items you want to hang, and to carve openings in the belt buckles.

• Set your carved and molded objects aside for about 5 days—until the clay dries and becomes chalky. Then sand any rough edges until smooth.

• Paint your pre-drawn design with Liquitex or poster paint—or any other opaque paint. Depending on your skill as a designer or painter, you can achieve amusing primitive effects or more formal

Heart locket, buttons, brooch and belt buckle are but a few of the handmade gifts that will please any age group. For a bazaar, each of the items can be made up in a complete range of colors, in both delicate and bold designs.

and elegant results. Allow paint to dry thoroughly, touch test it in about 24 hours.

• To give a flattering gloss to your work, as well as a protective coating, you can glaze the pieces with a variety of products. Brush on a polyurethane floor coating, available in hardware or paint stores, or use a fast-drying spray coating, such as Krylon. You can even use a clear nail polish, although this is not as durable as other coatings.

• If you'd like the experience of baking clay, there's a new and easy way to do this, too. Use Della Robbia Clay (also made by Sculpture House). It hardens in your oven at 250 degrees. It costs slightly less than Boneware Clay—less than $2 for a 3½-pound package. To work with it you follow the same steps outlined above, including the drying for 5 days or so. Then place in a *cold* oven, after painting, but before glazing. Set oven to 150 degrees and when the piece is warmed thoroughly, raise oven temperature to 250 degrees for 30 minutes to an hour, depending on the size and thickness of the piece. Leave the oven door open about two inches while baking.

That's all it takes to master ceramics without a kiln. The process is so easy to learn, the number of things to make so varied, this would make an ideal craft for your club when it comes time to make gifts for the bazaar booth.

Lady with the necklace (above) is one who "hangs loose" with her colored cord neck and legs. Try the same technique for a 20s version Romeo—even a Santa.

Scenic wall plaque (right) uses strips of applied clay for a 3-dimensional effect.

# Tree trims from fabric scraps

Remember the magic of childhood Christmas mornings? After absorbing the entire wonder of the Christmas tree, you sorted out one special ornament that, in a quiet way, became your very own. Long after you've forgotten details of the tree, that special ornament is still a happy memory.

At holiday time, children—often subconsciously—are storing away their own memories. That's the best reason to keep looking for new inspiration for tree trims and decorations. Those that you make are so often more memorable than those you can buy. And those that the children help make have a special meaning.

All ornaments shown are made chiefly of felt, fabric scraps and embroidery floss. Their special charm is that each takes on a personality according to the colors you use. Why shouldn't an angel have a fashionable print gown with a lace halo? And why shouldn't you see what each of the Wise Men looked like?

Load your tree with angels, pixies, Wise Men and Santas in a variety of brilliant colors, fabric designs, textures and trims. It will make an impact your children will remember for years to come.

**Patterns and directions begin on page 166**

Photography and designs/Gloria McNutt

# Glittering lighted hoops

**M**iniature lights are a holiday favorite, universally liked because they add such a fairyland quality to whatever they trim—from an avenue of trees along a city street to the more modest green garland hanging above your mantel. Cindy Hickok has designed yet another use for these tiny sparklers—by weaving them into a hanging ornament using ordinary rug yarn. It will be an eye-catching addition to your Christmas decor.

The supplies you need are few and easy to find. Besides the string of lights, you need a pair of wire hoops, 10 inches or so in diameter. If you can't find them in your local craft shops, make your own hoops from aluminum wire (9- or 12-gauge) held together with masking tape. Then get a hank of white rug yarn and you're ready to start.

The technique is simple enough—you braid four strands of yarn around the cord and hoops. Not much different from braiding a pigtail, except it takes four strands instead of three to braid a tube that will cover the plastic light cord and any imperfections (or masking tape) on the hoops.

Once you've made and displayed one of these lighted hoops, you'll probably get some hints from friends who would like one for a gift. Or you may be asked to make up some for the bazaar booth. This will give you a chance to try out any number of design variations. Try combining several colors, for instance. You'll find it works best if the colors are closely related, such as the deep red with purple in the illustration opposite. Note that part of the weaving uses the red only. If the colors are too contrasty, you get a dominant diagonal stripe that detracts from the lights.

Try combining several different textures—some fuzzy, some smooth; some nubby, some even. Use two or more strands of lightweight yarn as one—this gives further opportunity for color blending.

Besides using hoops perpendicular to each other, you can vary the design by using graduated sizes one within the other. Or by using more than a pair, arranged to form a globe. The variations possible for draping the covered light cord are endless; it can be bunched together at the top, hang in large loose loops, or hang straight down—or all of these. Chances are, before you put your supplies away until another year, you will have thought of several brand new uses for covered light cords!

Directions for making begin on page 164

New use for miniature lights: Cover the wires with yarn, drape gracefully from hoops. Hang in the front hallway to welcome your guests, or over the holiday buffet table to add a romantic glow.

Photography / Al Reagan      Design / Cynthia Hickok

# Quilling

. . .for lacy
Christmas
ornaments

Patterns and directions begin on page 158

*Quilling is a very old decorative art that originated with Italian nuns in the latter part of the Renaissance—1600s. The nuns rolled narrow strips of paper trimmed from books they were making around a bird feather quill (hence the name) to create scrolls, spirals, rosettes, flutes and a variety of other rolled shapes. By gluing these shapes together, they created designs to use for religious decorations.*

*The art of quilling spread from Italy to France and then to England, where in the early 19th century it suddenly became the rage. From there quilling quite naturally spread to America and enjoyed some popularity during the Victorian era. American women used quillwork to decorate sconces, boxes, picture frames and quite imaginatively used the tiny rolls of paper to create elaborately elegant valentines.*

*Today, there are not too many examples of early quillwork still existing in this country. However, the best and most complete collection can be seen at the Metropolitan Museum of Art in New York.*

Throughout the country the art of quilling—an ancient rolled paper technique used to create delicate designs—is reaching a renewed level of popularity. The reasons are simple: It's an inexpensive craft and anyone can do it.

Quilling is such a versatile craft that it lends itself to a myriad of unusual tree-trim and gift ideas. Follow our patterns; then try your own designs. Make four or five of each of the 14 basic shapes (directions follow) and try combining them in different ways. With imagination and this simple-to-learn technique, you can quill a whole collection of Christmas keepsakes—for yourself, your family and your friends.

### Easy to find supplies

Before doing any quilling, you'll need to gather some simple basic supplies—paper, glue, a ruler and a hat or corsage pin. (Ornamental supplies—sequins, studs, threads, cords, etc.—for the projects shown here are also handy to have on hand.)

You'll need ⅛-inch wide paper strips (white and colored) cut as straight as possible. Purchase an X-acto knife from a craft or art store and then use a ruler to guide your knife edge as you cut. Be sure to cut over cardboard so you won't mar the table.

The paper can be any type that will hold a curl—heavy typing paper, wrapping paper or good quality stationery. The weight (thickness) of the paper determines the diameter of the quilled shape. Avoid using inexpensive construction paper or any other paper that cracks easily. Some craft shops carry pre-

cut quilling papers. So, shop around a little before you cut your own.

You'll need a ruler to measure the exact length of a strip before it is rolled into a shape. (Different size shapes require different length strips—the bigger the shape, the longer the strip.) Tape the ruler to the edge of the work surface—saves hunting for it.

Next, you'll need paste or glue for closing circular shapes after the paper strip has been rolled, and for connecting one shape to another to form a design. If you select a paste, use a heavy, tacky craft paste that dries clear (Slomon's Velverette). If you prefer to use glue, select a white, tacky glue that dries clear (Elmer's or Sobo). Try to buy glue or paste in a container that ejects only a tiny drop at a time to the quillwork—no need for toothpicks. However, you still may want to have toothpicks on hand to reach those hard-to-get-to little places.

Although the nuns of Italy used a bird's quill to roll the paper strips, a hat or corsage pin is probably easier to find in your supply cabinet!

Tape waxed paper over your work table; this will keep quillwork from adhering to the table. Also, you can slip your design pattern underneath it, glue your quilled shapes together right over the pattern to get an accurate reproduction of the design.

### Helpful hints

Before making your first quilled shape, here are some helpful working hints:
- Always work neatly and with clean hands; paper easily shows grease and soil stains.
- Use glue and paste sparingly; even though it dries clear, it is shinier than the paper and will be somewhat noticeable.
- Tear the strips of paper to the proper length rather than cutting them. A torn edge is hardly noticeable when glued, while a cut edge shows.
- Use an empty egg carton to separate your quilled shapes before gluing them together. First, roll the number of each shape needed (following directions for each project); then, place each group of shapes in an individual egg holder. This spares you the frustration of searching for lost shapes.
- If your design starts twisting out of shape, carefully cut apart quilled shapes at the glued contact point, reglue. If a shape is too distorted, start over.
- When you arrange quilled shapes into a pleasing design of your own, draw a pattern of it before you glue the pieces together—then you'll have no trouble finding the correct spot for stray pieces.
- Feel free to use any kind of trim to emphasize your design: feathers, beads, dried flowers, seeds—anything is suitable so long as it can be glued and is not too heavy for the design. You may want to

Photography/Fred Carbone    Designs/Susan Sachs

A snowflake mobile (left) suspended over the dining room table is this year's new and unique holiday centerpiece.

Quilled fantasy flowers lend themselves to a wide variety of gift ideas: Frame and plaques (center) for decorating are easy to find at dime stores and craft shops.

For a special keepsake ornament, frame a Christmas tree in an embroidery hoop painted gold, decorate with sequins and braid.

**Patterns and directions begin on page 158**

80

spray a project with gold or silver paint to give a rich, sparkling effect. The snowflakes (pictured here) lend themselves to a gold or silver finish.

• Small, quilled peg shapes can be used on the back of some pieces being applied to a plaque or other flat surface, creating a raised effect.

• When you've finished a design, you may want to spray it with a clear plastic finish to give it extra protection and firmness, such as Varathane.

• When storing quillwork to reuse next year, layer cardboard or other flat, firm support between each piece. This will keep it from twisting out of shape.

## Basic rolling technique

To learn the basic rolling technique, start by making a loose circle (the most versatile of the 14 basic shapes). Grasp shank of the hat or corsage pin near the knob end between thumb and index finger of your right hand (see Fig. 1). Hold a 3-inch long strip of paper between thumb and index finger of your left hand. (The length of the strip will vary depending on how large you want the shape to be. But for practice purposes, a 3-inch strip will be fine.)

Start rolling the end of the paper around the pin either by moistening the end of the strip or making a soft fold in the paper. Roll the first two or three rounds very tightly; this will insure a neat center for the shape. For the remaining rounds, loosen up slightly, but keep the tension as even as possible for a neat, smoothly curving shape. Hold the shape secure until you have glued the end of the strip in position. Then, slip the shape off the pin. Your quill-

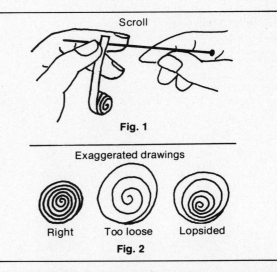

Scroll

**Fig. 1**

Exaggerated drawings

Right      Too loose      Lopsided

**Fig. 2**

work should look like the first shape shown in Fig. 2. If you are winding the paper lopsided or too loose, just keep practicing until you are satisfied that you have mastered the circle. Many of the other shapes are simple variations of the loose circle, so once you can make this shape, you'll have no trouble with the others.

## 14 basic shapes

The 14 basic shapes are used in the projects shown here. Not all of them are used in each project, but it might be a good idea to practice them before beginning. So, from the simple description and the drawing of each shape, practice making all 14 basic shapes. (Continue to use strips of paper 3 inches long for practicing.)

---

 **Loose Circle:** Roll your ⅛" strip of paper around the pin and glue it at the loose end. (See Basic rolling technique.)

 **Peg:** Roll a strip as tightly as possible around the pin and glue at the loose end.

 **Tear:** Make a loose circle. Pinch the circle at the point where the outside end was glued.

 **Eye:** Make a loose circle. Pinch the circle where the outside end was glued and the side opposite.

 **Triangle:** Make a loose circle. Pinch the loose circle at three points to form a triangle.

 **Diamond:** Make a loose circle Pinch the loose circle at four points to make a diamond.

**Pinched Heart:** Make a loose circle. Pinch it at the point where the outside end was glued. Then make an indent and pinch it to form the top of the heart.

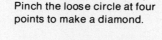 **Glued V:** Fold a strip of paper in the middle. Roll both ends outward toward the point of fold. Glue V closed a short distance from the point.

 **Open V:** Fold strip of paper in the middle. Roll both ends outward toward the point of fold. (Do not glue.)

 **Heart:** Fold strip of paper in the middle. Roll both ends inward. (Do not glue.)

**S Shape:** Roll strip halfway. Turn over and roll other end halfway. (Do not glue.)

**Scroll:** Roll both ends in toward the center. (Do not glue.)

 **Feather:** Fold strip slightly less than in half. Roll both ends in same direction. Glue as for Glued V if necessary to hold shape.

 **Cone:** Roll paper slightly on a diagonal along the pin and glue if necessary to hold shape.

# Easy to sew gifts for everyone

The gift you make has a special ingredient that money can't buy. It says you cared enough to spend your time and talent creating it.

Here is a roundup of things to sew that should cover almost everyone on your gift list—from a teacher to your favorite granddad—or granddaughter. And even for the clothing gifts, you only need to know the approximate sizes.

Search through your scrap bag or remnant drawer, and you'll probably find enough fabric to make several of these gifts. A small amount of stretch knit is all it takes to make a pair of shoe travel mitts; a small square of velveteen or fake leather is enough for an eyeglass case. And a half yard length is all you need for the main fabric in the patchwork tie.

**Patterns and directions begin on page 143**

Give this romantic-looking apron (left) to your favorite hostess. The ruffles cascade over the shoulders, across the front and up the back. Use giant rickrack to add a color accent and make a pair of matching hot-pad mitts to give with the apron—or as a separate gift.

Gather a variety of colored fabrics and embroidery floss to "paint" a landscape apron (opposite page): hills, trees, sun, two birds and one big bug. It's fun and a real conversation piece.

Photo/Mark Weingrad    Design/Jean Gillies

Design/Elizabeth Eaby

# Handmade gifts

Photography/Fred Carbone    Designs/Jean Gillies

Use four graduated squares to make a patchwork tie. You can cut each square of a single fabric (left tie), and make the tie with two different fabrics. Or you can cut each square in four sections, copying the tie on the right. This tie uses five coordinated fabrics, but you can get the same effect with three.

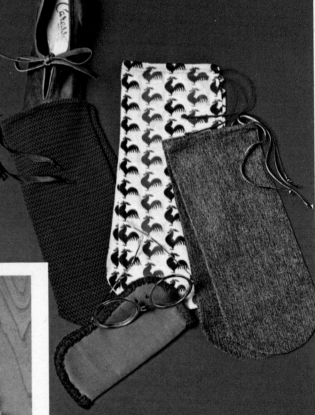

Present one or more sets of these shoe protector mitts to traveling friends. Use very stretchy fabric to fit a variety of shoe shapes. For the eyeglass case, use your imagination for fabric and color. We chose velveteen for both outside and lining and edged the case with braid.

Coordinate three fabrics to cover a table in patchwork. Use one design for the placemats and a similar one for the table runner. You can add variety by changing the position of colors from one block to the next, as we did. Use plain fabric at each end of table runner and for napkins.

**Patterns and directions begin on page 143**

Choose one—or both—of these cover-ups for a little girl. The red pinafore uses 66 yo-yos, each made separately, then sewed together. Ribbon ties hold it together at the sides. The Christmas tree apron is of sturdy denim with a ticking stripe. The practical trim is of rickrack and washable buttons outlined with chain-stitch embroidery.

Design/Elizabeth Eaby

Cushion design/Jean Gillies    Vest design/Mary M. Blanks

# Handmade gifts

A sports/utility vest and seat pad can work together or go their separate ways. The easy fitting vest has seven pockets to hold a variety of gear needed for fishing, hunting—or some carpentry work. The two bottom front pockets are zippered to keep things secure; beside them are tall narrow pockets—just right for eyeglasses or small flashlight. Two handy items you can't see are small swivel snaps. One is attached to a side seam for holding gloves, and another is sewed inside a zippered pocket for holding keys. The seat pad has a separate cover that zips over a foam square. A side pocket holds a newspaper—or the football program.

Make a petal skirt (below) of velveteen or corduroy to brighten the floor under your Christmas tree. Six overlapping petals circle the tree.

**Patterns and directions begin on page 143**

Design/Jean Gillies

You can quickly stitch up these two aprons for the men in your family. Use contrasting fold-over braid to bind the curved edges and pockets, and for making the apron ties and neck straps.

Design/Jean Gillies

# Stitched and stuffed art

Stitched and stuffed objects, so important in recent gallery and museum shows, point up that a skill as simple as sewing can result in beautiful art works. The current emphasis on quality handcrafts coupled with our almost fanatical return to nostalgia has resulted in both Fine Art and Folk Art exhibits that are outstanding.

Quilts originally made by our ancestors for the practical purpose of keeping warm are displayed today as treasured wall hangings. The modern quilts still have the remembered familiarity of "a piece of Pat's dress, Jim's shirt or the living room draperies." But the new synthetics and knit weaves along with the new sewing machine stitches have changed the modern quilt into something unique in the hands of an imaginative designer.

Stuffed toys appeared in history long before we thought of soft sculpture. In today's exhibit, the rag doll may be replaced by a humorous takeoff on a football player, the calico cat by one that looks astonishingly like the family's pet Siamese, or the Teddy bear by a stuffed "bird you can read."

The objects pictured here, collected from gallery shows across the country, are not meant to be copied line for line. Rather they're meant to stimulate your creativity. Leftover scraps or worn-out clothing, ribbons, feathers, old buttons and other hoarded materials from your scrap bag provide makings. A 10-cent needle or your trusty machine will sew an equally fine seam. The only limit to making stuffed art is what you can think up. "Art is a form of magic, turning ideas seen only in the mind into real images for others to see and touch."

Cat Pillow captures both the dignity and supple movements of a family pet; velvet upholstery fabric duplicates its furry pelt. Cotton stuffing, firmer than polyester fiberfill, holds the form upright.

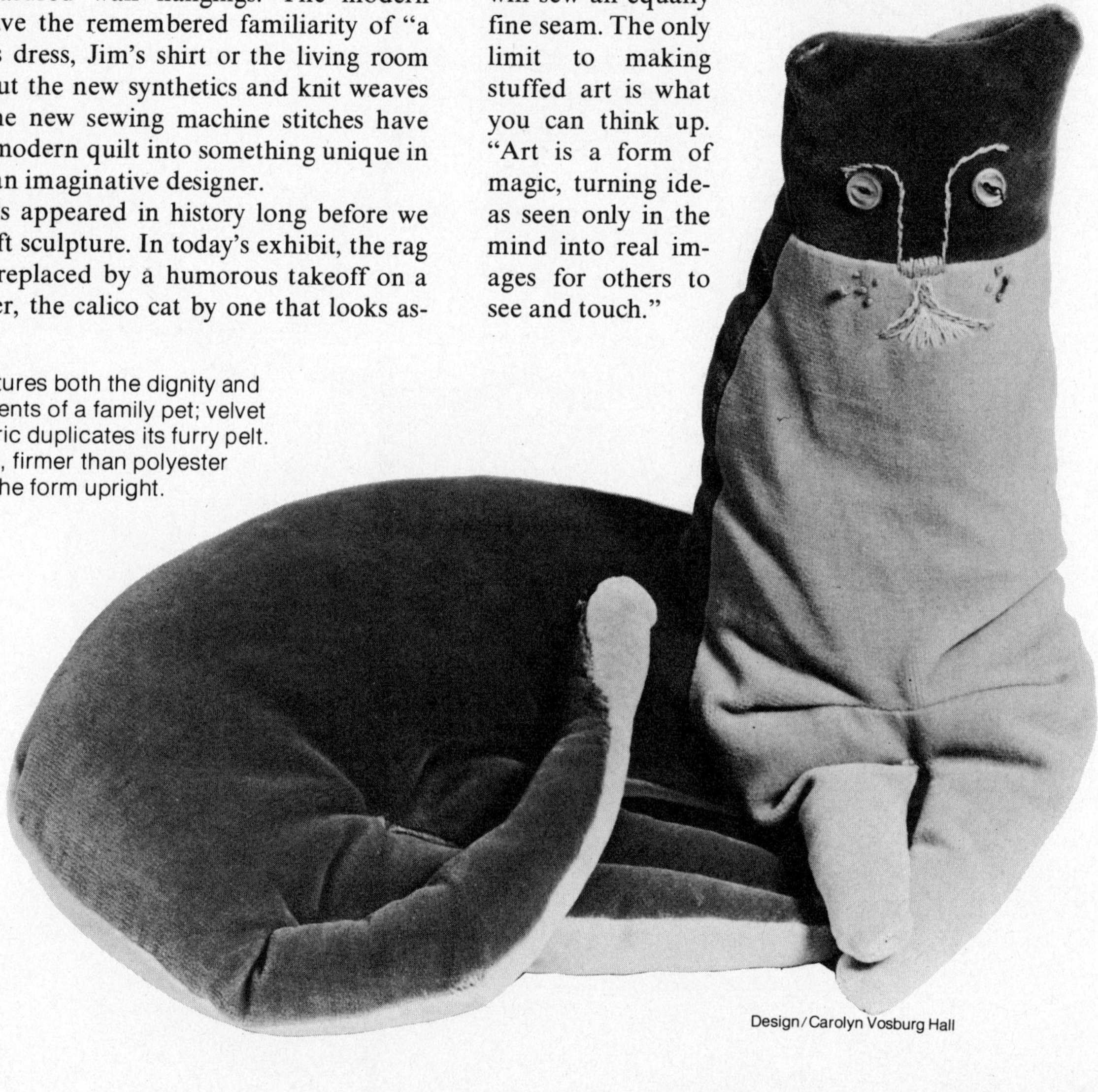

Design/Carolyn Vosburg Hall

Bird Book, only 8 inches high, becomes an educational toy with a report about flight, hand-lettered on its page-like wings. It's made of muslin fitted over a wire framework, then softly stuffed. Wire legs are wrapped with twine.

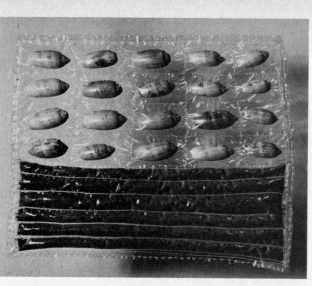

# Handmade gifts_____

Shells and Sand wall hanging (left) that pre-serves vacation memories will be a wel-come gift to your beach combing friends. Machine stitched pockets hold choice finds between two layers of clear plastic.

Pastoral Quilt (below) uses scraps of double-knit (edges don't ravel), machine stitched onto a fiberfilled square (work from the center out). The design has the fantasy-type storybook details that delight any child or adult.

Cowboy, Superman and Football Player (9″ tall) depict the he-man type favorites with supersized bodies, humorously topped with pinheads. A good gift for boys.

Design/George Landino

People Pillows—or are they dolls? Castles, kings and princesses inspired the designs representing people in a simplified way. Embroidery floss defines the features, adds texture.

Design/Pat St. Cyr

# Old denim

## One man's junk is another man's treasure

*Everytime someone gets ready to do a good clean-out job in the house or barn, somebody comes around screaming, "Don't throw that away. They're paying fabulous prices for that stuff." Where are all these people who are paying those "fabulous prices" for barn siding and mason jars and old bottles, rusty nails, wavy window panes, hand-hewn beams, and—are you ready for this one—worn and faded blue denim?*

*Right there in* Time: *Saks Fifth Avenue is selling faded denim jackets for $26, and bikinis made of old denim go for $20.*

*Odd as it seems, there's real justice in placing such value on genuinely faded blue denim. (It seems they try to simulate the faded effect, but imitations don't command the price of the real thing.) In order to achieve real "patina," blue denim needs to do a lot of bending in the sun and whipping in the wind. It needs to be dunked in farm ponds and ground into the slag of playgrounds. It needs to fall from horses or motor-cycles or bicycles a few dozen times, and be forgotten on a fence post for a few weeks. It should kick around in a dusty pickup truck a while. Most of all it needs to be soaked repeatedly in sweat. It has to lie in dirty laundry piles on damp cellar floors and hang for long spells on clothes lines. It needs to be shortened and lengthened again and mildewed in mending piles and be nursed back to health with patches.*

*Then and only then does a garment of blue denim have real integrity. And believe me, it's worth more than any city slicker can pay.* —Pat Leimbach

**Patterns and directions begin on page 154**

Photography/Mark Weingrad  Pants/Made by Cheri Huseby

For dress-up occasions, this long skirt is paired with a fitted jacket. Embroider your own design on the skirt hem, and dress up the jacket with rhinestone buttons. (See back view on next page.)

For shopping or sightseeing, here's a nifty recycled denim jacket and pants outfit topped with a patched beret. To make the jacket, turn one of your old cotton shirts inside out and cover with denim patches.

Rhinestones form a streaking star on the back of this jacket (above). These repeat the glitter of rhinestone buttons used on the front. (See page 92.)

For casual dressing (right), turn strips of faded denim into this easy-to-make unlined vest; add recycled pockets. Wear it with three-quarter-length pants that have your personalized embroidery on one cuff.

**Patterns and directions begin on page 154**

Denim—as in blue jeans—is the fabric darling of the world right now. It's sturdy and durable. It does fade, soften and show signs of wear, but nobody cares—everybody prefers it that way. Second-hand denim has the status of an antique; people are paying higher prices for an outfit of patched-up old denim that's creatively trimmed with embroidery, nailheads, sequins or rhinestones.

City prices for worn, used jeans keep rising, while supplies are dwindling. Second-hand jeans are snapped up by creative people who want to recycle them.

In a family of teens, however, jeans keep piling up. When you can't cut down jeans to fit anyone else, and you have enough rag rugs, what next?

Pants/Made by Cheri Huseby

Rock-collector's tote: Design/Margaret White

Looking for a carry-all tote? Then make your own from old denim. Open-top patchwork bags are easy—patches can be stitched right to the lining. For a shoulder bag, make a tote with a pocket flap (center). Surprise a rock collector with an over-the-shoulder tote (shown on the ground) made from an old pant leg.

Delight a youngster—or even a grownup—with denim dolls (right). They look cute as twins, but even one makes a fun gift.

Design/Jean Gillies

Embroidered quilt/Made by Olive M. McMillen    Crazy patch quilt/Made by Pauline Isom

Well, our advice is: Don't throw the old jeans out! Join the movement and recycle them. Teenagers love 'em. To help inspire you (or them), we've gathered ideas from around the country—and we've added a few of our own. Some great gift ideas.

For a city friend, you might even gift-wrap a box of plain old jeans. Present it, along with the ideas shown here, and let the recipient create her (or his) own recycled gems.

Make a quilt from faded denim. The child's crazy patch quilt with monogrammed pocket is the quickest to make. Use Father's old jeans and Grandfather's overalls. If you have more time, try an embroidered memory quilt. The one shown here has 165 blocks, each 5″ square, half of them embroidered. Personalize your memory quilt with embroidered blocks to remind you of vacation places, special holidays, favorite songs and family birth dates. Work in scraps from a favorite shirt or dress.

**Patterns and directions begin on page 154**

# New uses for old laces

Chances are you have a dresser drawer or a cardboard box in the attic harboring accumulations of hand crocheted or tatted doilies and miscellaneous laces. Some of these are so exquisitely made that they deserve to be preserved. But how to use them?

Laces belong to a different pace of living, a time of polished furniture and formal parlors. Part of the charm of their antique handwork is in the way these pieces remind us of the women who created them. We are, at last, truly learning to appreciate the hand and needle arts which have been disregarded for years. Flea markets, antique sales and auctions are featuring old laces and are a source of fascinating finds. It's time to empty those boxes and drawers and to once again enjoy rich heritage of handwork by making artistic uses of old laces.

If you are fortunate enough to have inherited a collection then you're ready to proceed on any of the projects shown in these pages. If you have none yourself, locating some is your first adventure. Try your older relatives—laces are easily mailed. Many a grandmother will be delighted that you actually *care* about her long-neglected bits of handwork.

Department stores carry lacy ribbons, edgings and yardage which combine beautifully with handmade pieces if your supply is limited. Finally, of course, if your talents extend to crochet, tatting, knitting, or any of the other needle arts, you can make your own. Many women still make lace, often in great abundance. Contact a senior citizens' center to locate needlework enthusiasts. Some women will produce and sell the work directly or through church bazaars and specialty shops. A single ad in your local newspaper may bring to light unexpected sources of needlework.

There are many delightful ways to let these valued remnants of the past become a part of today. The intricately detailed hand arts bring a nostalgic beauty when combined with new materials and new ways of working. In these pages are some examples of how stitchery artists have used old needlework in contemporary design. It is important to put this handwork out where it can be seen and enjoyed. Since it will only yellow and deteriorate stored in a dresser drawer, you might as well let it age where you can admire it.

It is not necessary to be knowledgeable about the needle arts to appreciate and enjoy them. It is almost a certainty, however, that as you work with them and learn to recognize and identify various methods, your curiosity and appreciation will make you an eager student. For instance, did you know

Dove of Peace uses a patchwork of
delicate laces sandwiched between two
layers of felt. Cut out bird and leaf shapes
fom the top layer; insert lace to fill the
openings. Lace is enhanced by the color
of the bottom layer. Whip-stitch the two
layers to hold the lace in place. Use
couching to emphasize the bird outline.

Cover eggshells with lace for truly
unusual Christmas tree ornaments.
Paint emptied shells with bright colors
to complement the off-whites of the lace.
Use small lace pieces—they're easier
to mold to an egg shape; attach with glue.
This is a way to salvage the good
parts of damaged laces.

that doilies, usually circular forms, were made as
decoration and protection to be used under glasses,
bowls or vases? The name came from a seventeenth
century draper, a Mr. Doyley or Doily. He appar-
ently covered so much of London with his work that
any cover became known as a "Mr. Doily." That
was finally shortened to "doily."

Antimacassars came in many shapes and sizes,
and originally they served a very specific function.
Macassar was a hair dressing or hair oil for men
and the anti-Macassar was feverishly designed to
protect the parlor furniture. Under the pretense of
decoration, the anti-Macassar was placed at head
level on chairs and sofas and could easily be removed for washing. Soon companion pieces were made
for the arms of sofas or chairs. As time went by, antimacassars became more profuse, more extrava-
gantly detailed. They provided protection for the
furniture as well as a socially desirable means of ex-
hibiting the homemakers' handiwork skills.

There are geometric patterns in doilies as varied
and elegant as snowflakes. And they were made by
every conceivable form of needlework. Dresser
scarves and vanity sets were created by crochet, tatting and knitting. Along with these, drawn-thread
work and cut openwork offered rich and varied designs. In drawn-thread work, either warp or weft
threads were snipped and removed. This left open
areas of threads which were then knotted and
stitched into patterns. In cut openwork, both warp
and weft threads were cut, knots and stitches added.

Bobbin laces were made by using threads wound
on bobbins, which milady darted, twisted, crossed,
and knotted with the nimbleness of a cat's-cradle
magician. Needle laces were worked over skeletal
threads, using only a needle for the stitches and
knots, which gradually grew into a small and ex-
quisite unit of off-the-loom weaving.

Each lace method has its own special characteris-
tic appearance. Elegant white-on-white satin
stitches subtly trimmed hand towels and pillow-
cases. More often than not, the tablecloth, pillow-
case or dresser scarf was simply a vehicle for extending a homemaker's skills and creative impulses.

You really need know nothing about the background of lacework, but if working with old pieces
makes you envious, the library is an excellent
source of reference and instruction. And no matter
how limited your experience in stitchery and needle
arts, you will find new adventures and ways in
which to apply your skills. We give you some ideas
to get you started, but rely on your own imagination to find new places for old laces.

Give festive flair to a simple wrap-around skirt (right) with an array of lace doilies and antimacassars. White cording was used to unify this design, but other trims also can be used.

Laces are particularly applicable to all kinds of quilts. For the crib quilt, (below), velveteen was cut to size, lace shapes pinned in position and sewn. Quilting follows the flower forms.

Photography/Fred Carbone    Design/Muriel Leafstet

Bits and pieces of lace (far left) can be used dramatically. For this wall hanging, circular lace doilies are used for flower centers, linear lace patterns for stems.

"San Francisco Summer House" (left) uses rectangular lace forms, circular doilies and portions of salvaged place mats and edgings.

Photography/Gayle Smalley    Designs/Jean Ray Laury

Pillow tops (left) provide endless possibilities for the use of laces and needlework. Although these pillows are not likely to survive family-room pillow fights, they add a lovely touch to Grandmother's rocker or a favorite easy chair.

Angel in handsewn wall hanging is all the more angelic for its use of bits of lace applique and embroidery. The halo uses a large crochet doily and has an applique over the worn linen center.

Photography/Gayle Smalley    Designs/Jean Ray Laury

# Handmade gifts

A combination of new and old laces were used to make this spectacular dirndl skirt with bib— a wonderful keepsake gift idea for a special friend or relative.

These simple dolls(below) use bits of crochet, tatting and laces. Dolls made with cotton fabric and stuffed with Dacron are machine washable; felt is a good choice for colorful dolls.

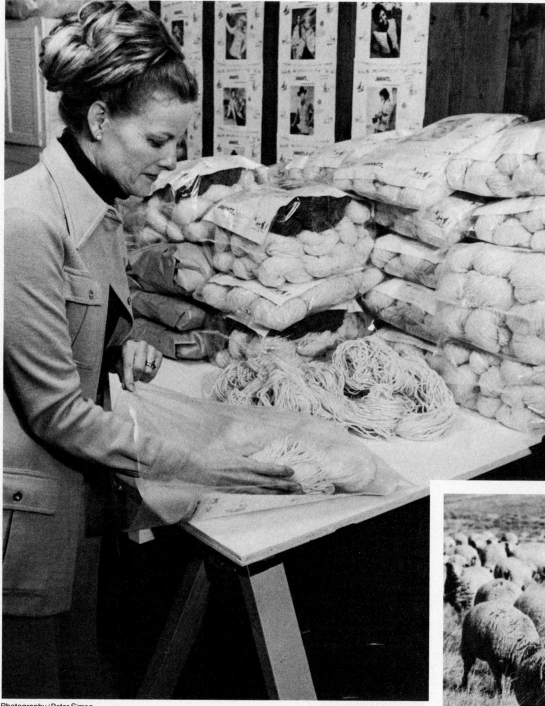

Janet Mysse (above)
assembles knitting kits in her
basement workroom.

The Mysses raise Columbia
sheep exclusively (right); it's an
all-purpose breed used for both
wool and meat.

# Knitting ...from a hobby to a business

**I**f you're a non-stop knitter and you are surrounded by thousands of sheep, the combination could put you in business. That happened to Janet Mysse of Rosebud County, Montana, three years ago.

Janet has been knitting since she was in high school. "People wouldn't know me if I didn't go to a meeting with a sackful of knitting and yank it out," she says. "Through the years, I've picked up many helpful ideas that aren't in any direction books. I finally looked at all those sheep and decided to put my knitting skills and the wool together." That's how Janknits, based on do-it-yourself kits, began.

For her business, Janet designs original patterns for such things as sweaters, ponchos and afghans, then packages the directions with enough yarn for an individual project. Kits are sold primarily by mail order from her basement workroom on the ranch. Each year she puts out a catalog (for which she charges 25¢), complete with pictures of the sheep and ranch. "We like to give the business a home-grown look," she says. "People seem to enjoy seeing what the sheep business is like."

The yarn, which she also sells by the pound or skein, comes from the Mysse sheep. Janet buys wool at the going price from the Cherry Creek Sheep Company (owned by husband Sivert and his two sisters). She ships the wool to Boston for scouring, then it goes on to Maine where it's made into yarn. It comes back to the ranch for packaging. All Mysse sheep are white, so Janet buys the dark wool used for pattern effects from other producers.

The finished yarn has some lanolin left in (Janet calls this oiled yarn), and it is the natural wool color. This type of yarn is the kind used for knitting warm, water-resistant fisherman-type designs that are inspired by the traditional handknit sweaters of Ireland. (Legend suggests each sweater was different so that if a fisherman drowned, he could be identified by his sweater.)

"Even though the yarn is off-white in color, you can wear these sweaters a long time before they look dirty and have to be washed," says Janet.

"I think a sweater should be warm and look nice for 20 years," Janet says. Since the fisherman-style sweater has become a classic fashion, you could consider one an investment.

Janet's business brings her in contact with women all over the country. Some write to thank her for creating such a nice design, while others comment on the lovely wool. One woman sent a finished sweater for Janet's approval. A few women write questions about knitting problems unrelated to the Janknits kits; they just feel she is an authority. "These contacts bring me recognition," says Janet. "Even though we show little profit so far because we use earnings to expand the business, I have the *feeling* of success. And that alone is a great reward."

# Five things to knit

Man's pullover sweater (above) worn by the Mysses' neighbor, Howard Newman, has the same pattern on both front and back. The neckline ribbing is folded to the inside for double thickness and to give a firm edge. Like all of Janet Mysse's designs, the sweater has raglan sleeves, so there's no trouble with fit at the shoulders.

Woman's wrap-around sweater (right), worn by Johnna Newman (she's married to Howard), is tied with a knitted belt. This heavy outdoor sweater features a double-moss pattern and has a roll collar. The border design along the bottom edges of the coat and the sleeves is worked with dark yarn.

Pillow and afghan (above) are done in unique fisherman-type designs. The 16-inch-square pillow, with its patterned front and plain back, is knitted on circular needles (decreases at the corners make it square). The 60- by 44-inch, no-seam, fringed afghan is knitted all in one piece. Included in its design are the popcorn-ladder, double-moss and bramble patterns.

Child's pullover sweater (left) can be made for either a boy or girl. Sivert Mysse Jr. and Marni Erickson wear theirs while playing in a wooded ridge overlooking the ranch. Double ribbing makes the neckline firm, and the raglan sleeves are typical of Janet's designs. The fisherman-type design on the front is repeated on the back.

**Directions for making
begin on page 168**

# That extra joy of childhood giving: I made it myself

**W**hat gifts can 6- to 12-year-olds make for parents and grandparents, brothers and sisters, teachers and friends?

Children are at their creative best when you put a selection of things you find around the house in front of them: old magazines, bits of yarn and string, fabric scraps, modeling clay, glue, dried flowers or weeds—even potatoes! The magic of imagination takes over and transforms these humble materials into tangible tokens for sharing.

Ideas on these pages are not offered as designs to be copied exactly—they're starters. As children start working, new ideas will pop into their minds and they will carry them in completely different directions from the original.

## MIRRORS

**Materials:** Pocket mirrors (available in hobby shops); "clay" (recipe below); waxed paper; acrylic or tempera paints (optional).

**Directions:** Make the clay from 4 cups flour, 1 cup salt, 1½ cups water. Mix ingredients; knead for a few minutes until smooth. Use immediately or store in refrigerator in plastic wrap.

Spread waxed paper over children's working area. Flatten a handful of clay on the waxed paper and press mirror into it. Use additional clay to decorate the surface—such as the leaves around the hand mirror (a popsicle stick reinforces the handle). Use fork or toothpicks to create embossed designs in clay. For a hanging mirror, insert hairpin or paper clip in back while clay is soft.

Place mirrors on a cake rack for baking (if clay sticks to waxed paper, bake with paper on and remove excess when dry). Bake small items at 350° for 1 hour until dry; large items at 250° for 6 hours until dry. When cool, paint if desired.

You'll find that once the children start working with the dough, they will become so engrossed with the possibilities, they'll keep right on working after the mirror project is finished!

# Handmade gifts

## PAPERWEIGHTS

**Materials:** Glass or clear plastic caster cups; light-weight cardboard; plaster of Paris; felt; white glue; flat items for designs: photographs, small nails and washers, pressed flowers, etc.

**Directions:** Cut cardboard into shapes which fit into the caster cups. Glue the photographs, pressed flowers or hardware designs onto cardboard; let dry. Place cardboard face down into cup; fill with plaster of Paris mixed according to directions on box. If more than one cup is to be filled, add 1 teaspoon vinegar to ¼ cup plaster to slow the setting time. Let dry. Glue a circle of felt to bottom to cover plaster surface.

Older children can make these paperweights by themselves; younger ones will need help with cutting cardboard to fit cups and with mixing plaster.

## MAGNETIC BOARD

**Materials:** 8″ length of 1 × 1½″ pine board; screws for hanging; sandpaper; wood stain; self-adhesive magnetic tape (in 30″ lengths from hobby shops).

**Directions:** Drill a hole in each end of board for screws. (This will have to be done by an adult unless child has had experience with a drill.) Sand wood until smooth; apply wood stain (or make your own from 2 tblsp. instant coffee and 2 tsp. water).

## SACHET BALLS

**Materials:** Large-size tea ball; crisp fabric; yarn; lavender, spices or scented soap.

**Directions:** Open tea ball and fill with lavender, spices or coarsely grated soap. Remove metal chain, substitute yarn for hanging. Place filled tea ball in center of a 10″ square of fabric—we used colorful cottons. Gather at top and tie with yarn.

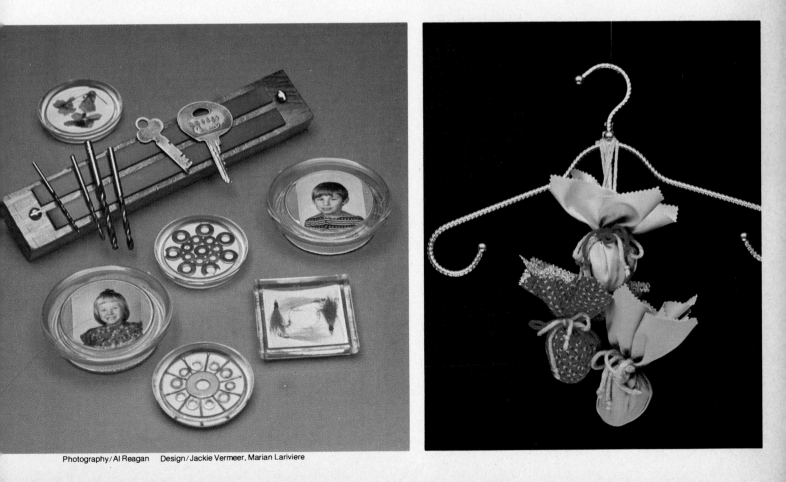

Photography/Al Reagan    Design/Jackie Vermeer, Marian Lariviere

## POTATO BEADS

**Materials:** Potatoes; apple corer; tapestry needle; heavy cord or carpet warp; food coloring; salt; beads; small safety pins.

**Directions:** For dried beads (the dark ones): use apple corer to remove "cores" from potatoes. Then, slice into round beads (these will shrink to about half their original size and turn dark as they dry). String on cord and hang to dry.

For salt-packed beads: Peel and cut potatoes into thick slices, then cut triangular shapes. Pack beads in table salt and leave for two days. Then, wash off salt. String, using small beads as spacers. Hang to dry until hard. Salt packing retains the white color; if the beads are rinsed again after drying, they will darken slightly.

To color beads: Peel and cut as above; soak for several minutes in food coloring mixed with water; then pack in salt for several days.

Add a small safety pin to each end of the string to serve as a clasp.

## MAGAZINE BEADS

**Materials:** Colored pages from magazines; toothpicks; white glue; carpet warp; spray lacquer.

**Directions:** Cut colorful magazine pages into triangles—the length of the page and about 1″ wide at the bottom. Lay toothpick across bottom of triangle and roll up. Dip tip of paper in glue and press in place. Let dry, then slip off toothpick. String on carpet warp; then spray completed necklace with lacquer.

## MINIATURE BEAD VASES

**Materials:** Glass beads; waxed paper; white glue; dried straw flowers.

**Directions:** Place a bead on waxed paper (this allows easy removal of bead after glue dries). Fill hole with white glue, insert straw flowers. If bead is small, glue to cardboard base for stability. Young children will need a large bead (from a bead stringing set) for their arrangement.

# EMBROIDERY HOOP PICTURES

**Materials:** Hoops; fabric or old white sheet; liquid starch; colored chalk; decorative hangers.

**Directions:** Cut fabric several inches larger than hoop; lay over inner ring and push outer ring into place. Paint area inside hoop with liquid starch; draw design with chalk on wet background. Pull fabric taut again and let dry. Trim excess fabric; add decorative hanger.

# CORK-FLOWER PICTURES

**Materials:** Sheet cork; straw flowers; felt scraps; white glue; picture hangers.

**Directions:** Cut cork to desired shape and size. Arrange flowers in place. Cut felt "bow or "vase." Apply glue both over stems (in area that will be covered by felt) and felt strips. Attach hanger to back. For large pictures, use lightweight cardboard backing to give extra strength.

# CORK-FELT COASTERS

**Materials:** Sheet cork; permanent felt markers; felt in assorted colors; white glue.

**Directions:** Cut cork into 3″ squares or circles. Draw designs with felt markers. Cut 3½″ squares or circles of colored felt. Glue cork onto felt. Very young children can make the cork a solid color rather than try multicolored designs.

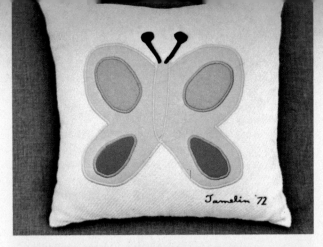

If there's a youngster in the house, there's an artist in residence, says Mrs. Esmond McNutt of Visalia, California. Even before they learn to write, most kids will draw objects they've seen. Mrs. McNutt proves the universal appeal of her children's designs by turning their art into bright and amusing one-of-a-kind pillows and plaques.

"I carefully trace the children's finished designs. All it takes, really, is fabric scraps; you can applique the designs by machine. Use a zigzag stitch—it will keep the edges of the fabric from turning up, and you won't have to turn edges under before stitching."

The pillows have been so well received that Gloria McNutt now "commissions" drawings from her children, ages 7 and 10.

"When we're making an odd-shaped pillow, first we talk about what the shape reminds them of. Triangular and round pillows inspire the most interesting drawings."

The drawings can also be translated into wood, as the McNutts discovered in planning gifts to please two grandmothers.

Butterfly, zinnia, sun, elephant, owl, house or car—all of these familiar objects take on a charming simplicity when the uninhibited hands of children use them in designs. When appliqued onto pillows of all sizes and shapes, they look like Folk Art at its best.

# Children's designs have extra appeal

# Handmade gifts

Photography/Gloria McNutt

Next time you're called upon to be your children's art critic, consider the possibilities. The pillows are easy to make with materials you already have on hand, and you'll be preserving memories of your children's early years. All on your Christmas list will be pleased with a gift that is so much a part of you and your children.

You could build an unusual bazaar booth around gifts and decorations made from children's art—a sure way to attract attention!

## PILLOWS

**Materials:** Covering fabric, tracing paper, fabric scraps (felt is good), mercerized cotton thread, cording for seam (optional), pillow form.

**Directions:** Measure pillow form. From covering fabric, cut front and back to fit pillow form, allowing for ½" seam. Carefully trace drawing on paper to use as a pattern. Pin pattern to fabric scraps; cut two patterns. Using machine zigzag stitch, applique the design pieces onto both front and back of covering fabric. Pin front and back cover, right sides together. (If you are using cording, it should be inserted at this time.) Machine stitch three sides of rectangular shape pillow or two-thirds of circular shape. Turn covers to right side; insert pillow form. Close open seam with small hand stitches.

Grandma

G is for granting us wishes we make.
R is for the **really** special cards you get us.
A is for **always** loving us.

N is for **never** scolding us.

D is for the delicious hamburgers you make us.
M is for the memories you have given us to treasure.
A is for all the things you do for us.

# GRANDMOTHERS' PLAQUE

**Materials:** Background fabric, felt for plaque backing (optional). Wood: rectangle of scrap wood (¼″ plywood) for background; ½″ and ⅜″ pine pieces (different thicknesses add interest) for figures in plaque. Staple gun, white glue, wood putty, jig saw (electric or hand). Plastic spray (crayon and ink tend to run with brush-on finishes): velvet or satin finish (we used New Finish Clear Varnish by Major Paint Co., Torrance, California). Screw eyes, picture wire.

**Directions:** Cut fabric to cover backboard by measuring wood piece and adding 1″ to each side for wrap around. Cover board with fabric, folding over edges and stapling to back. (Optional: glue felt to back for a more finished look.) Set aside. Fill any holes in pine pieces with wood putty. Glue artwork to pieces with white glue. Roll out wrinkles. Cut out artwork with a hand or electric jig saw. Cover all pieces with plastic spray—one coat is enough. Glue artwork into position on front of covered board. Use white glue and weight with a book until completely dry. Twist screw eyes into back of board and attach wire for hanging. (Two small blocks of wood, glued to bottom back of plaque will keep it from tilting on the wall.)

# Make the toys you give

Design: Jean Ray Laury

**A** handmade toy gives double pleasure. Not only does it delight the child who receives it, but it also brings real satisfaction to the adult who made it. The more creative the toy, the more the pleasure.

A good toy is one that expands the potential of children. It need not be elaborate, expensive or complex. Children look for challenge, for the opportunity to discover and to explore. As a by-product, they develop muscles and dexterity through the manipulation of objects; they develop number and color concepts and learn size and shape relationships. Most commercial toys contribute little to these needs because "playing" often becomes mere turning a switch and changing batteries. Given the materials (and some adult help as needed), children themselves are imaginative and successful toymakers.

Making toys is part of the adult world too. It's the next best thing to recapturing childhood. Certainly, a successful toymaker needs to have some personal feeling of what it is like to play with the toy he makes.

To stimulate this creative urge in both children and adults, Jean Ray Laury and Ruth Law have written a book on Handmade Toys. The toys are designed with wit and humor, using scraps of this and that. There are suggestions for the man who is handy with hammer and saw as well as for the woman who likes to sew.

We've selected a few toys from the book as suggestions for Christmas giving. The designs, though simple to duplicate, are meant to be used as a springboard for creating your own.

Design: Char Aiden

Simple wood blocks (top, left) are cut from 2 × 2″ pine, sanded, lightly stained and left to dry. Designs in bright colors are painted or silk-screened onto card-weight paper, then glued to the blocks. Protect the designs with a final coat of clear finish.

This stuffed horse (left) can gallop, canter or pace. The movable legs are cut, stitched and stuffed separately, then attached to the body by pulling yarn all the way through the legs as well as the body. Jaunty mane and tail of yarn give the finished toy the look of a spirited horse.

Handmade dolls are sure to please, no matter what they're made of. Ruth Law uses stretch knit fabrics (salvaged from children's outgrown clothes) stuffed with polyester fiberfill. For facial features and hair, she uses yarns, buttons, felt scraps, embroidery details.

Trojan horse is a toy that teaches—how Troy was taken by soldiers hidden in a wooden horse. Body has three layers—two outside layers of ¼'' plywood (door cut in one side), center layer of ¾'' pine with hiding place cut out of it. Legs of ⅜'' plywood are nailed to body. Horse is 12'' tall, soldiers 1½''.

Photography: Gayle Smalley   Designs: Ruth Law

Red circus wagon (above) trimmed with a white star-like design measures 7'' tall. Two plywood sides are temporarily nailed together for sawing (assures identical designs). Wheels are sliced from 2'' birch dowels.

Nursery rhyme toy (left) features the old woman who lives in a bright, felt shoe—with a Masonite inner sole! Her many children are cut out of 5/16'' pine and painted with bright enamel colors. Roof line measures 7''.

# How to make your own "cut glass" candles

You've seen them in the stores—those candles which resemble to the last facet a piece of treasured antique cut glass. But do you know it's possible to duplicate your own treasures in wax?

A fairly recent innovation in professional candlemaking is the use of a silicone compound called RTV (room temperature vulcanizing) Molding Rubber. With RTV it's possible to reproduce almost any object of reasonable size in minute detail.

RTV Molding Rubber may not be available in your local retail store but we have located two mail order suppliers: Cathy's Candle Cupboard (415 E. Highland Ave., Iowa City, Iowa 52240) and Berton Plastics (P.O. Box 101, Warminster, Pa. 18974). Each of these firms can supply RTV in one-pound packages and the cost is around ten dollars. Ask for General Electric RTV 700 or Dow-Corning Silastic 3116. Or write General Electric Silicones Div., RTV Section, Waterford, N.Y. 12188, for a list of distributors.

If you follow instructions carefully, you'll find it relatively easy to make a successful rubber mold from this material. An RTV mold will last through hundreds of wax pourings without losing any detail or finished candle quality. Cut-glass objects are the most popular, but not the only suitable models for rubber molding. "Miniature animals, statues and novelties of all sorts can be duplicated in wax with RTV molds," says William E. Webster, author of *The Complete Book of Candlemaking*.

For step-by-step instructions we are using an antique toothpick holder and a cut-glass bowl. The latter will become a hanging candle. You may substitute a drinking glass, vase, globe or whatever cut glass (or imitation) you have; the principle of making the mold is the same.

Candlemaking is not difficult but, if you've never tried it, here's a quick review lesson before you start your rubber mold candle: Buy wax at a craft or candle shop; don't use supermarket paraffin. Melt wax in a double boiler—never over direct heat. Add color chips or liquid color (also from the craft shop) to the wax after it is melted. Use a candy thermometer and let your wax heat to about 210°. There is no need to grease a rubber mold, as you would a metal mold.

## TO MAKE AN RTV MOLD YOU'LL NEED:

Glass or plastic cutting board
RTV compound (including slow
  catalyst)
  (also need "fast catalyst"
  for second technique)
Bowl for mixing
Two tablespoons
Floral or modeling clay
Rubber band
Razor blade or sharp knife
Small towel
Container to fit over model
  (needed only for first technique
  shown)
Small drill and awl

Photography/Al Reagan   Designs/William Webster

### STEP 1
Apply floral clay to the edge of the top rim of the model. This will hold it fast to your work surface. Peel off excess clay so that it does not protrude beyond the edge.

### STEP 2
Turn the model upside down and press it firmly to the work surface.

### STEP 3
A "mother mold" can be any container large enough to fit over your model with ½″ space at top and sides. Here you see a plastic container with the bottom sawed off.

### STEP 4
Press floral clay around top edges of the mother mold.

STEP 1

STEP 2

STEP 3

STEP 4

## STEP 5

Turn mother mold upside down but, before adhering edge to work surface, measure it against the model and draw a line inside and outside to indicate the level of the ½″ margin at top.

## STEP 6

Clean the model thoroughly to remove all fingerprints from handling or they will be reproduced in the mold.

## STEP 7

Center the mother mold over the model and press it firmly to the work surface.

## STEP 8

Measure 10 tablespoons of RTV compound into the mixing bowl. (Used here is an inexpensive dog food bowl that can be reused.)

## STEP 9

Measure 1 tablespoon of "slow catalyst" from the tube into the bowl and mix thoroughly. The more catalyst you use the faster the mold will cure, but 10 to 1 is the recommended ratio.

### STEP 10

Pour the mixture into the mother mold, letting it run down over the model.

### STEP 11

Continue pouring until the compound reaches the ½" margin mark you made. Let the poured compound stand 24 hours for curing. Clean mixing bowl by letting compound cure, then peel it out.

### STEP 12

The next day, cut the excess material from the top of the mother mold with a sharp knife or blade so that it is level with the top of the poured RTV.

### STEP 13

With a small saw or sharp blade, slit the side of the mother mold to remove it from the cured rubber.

### STEP 14

With a sharp knife, slit rubber mold down the side and halfway around the bottom of the model. Try to cut along a line in the pattern of the model. This is not essential but it will make for a neater seam line on your candles.

STEP 10

STEP 11

STEP 12
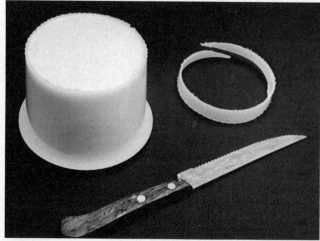

STEP 13
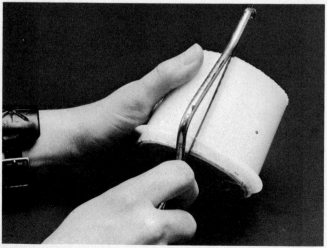

STEP 14
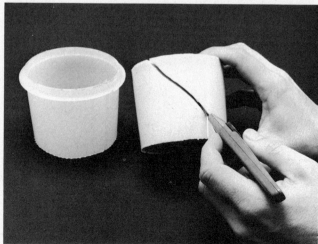

## STEP 15
Open the slit rubber mold and the model will be easy to remove.

## STEP 16
Drill small hole through the center bottom of the rubber mold from the inside. This will provide space for the candle wick.

## STEP 17
Insert the wick, using an awl or thin guide wire with a flattened end to push the wick through the hole in the rubber. Lay a pencil or slim rod across the top of the mold and fasten the wick to it by knotting or twisting. Put the rubber mold back in the mother mold.

## STEP 18
Place a heavy rubber band around the mother mold, near the bottom, to keep the slit from opening. Pour wax at 210°. Repour as often as wax recedes in the mold—but do not pour higher than the original level.

## STEP 19
After candle hardens—3 hours and up, depending on size—remove it from the mold. It practically pops out and the pattern of the model is reproduced in every detail. Rubber molds can be used again.

STEP 15

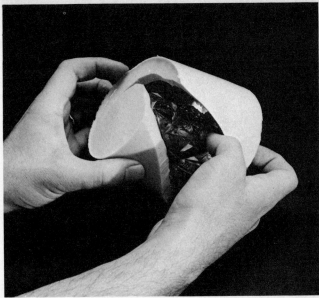

STEP 17

STEP 16

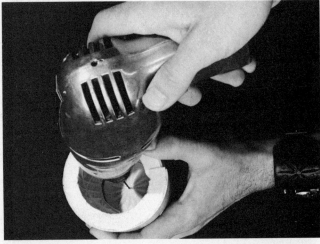

STEP 18

STEP 19

121

# For a gift that's sure to please
# Give a collectible

Photography/Bernie Cleff

# Give a collectible

If things of the past appeal to you, yet you've never felt rich enough to collect antiques, you might have a pleasant surprise in store. "Country antiques," things your not-too-distant ancestors used and probably handed down to members of the family, are the current rage among collectors.

Country antiques include furniture and farm implements, of course. But the richest vein in this category is the varied assortment of kitchenware—pots, pans, kettles, strainers and the rest. Humble objects all, but dearly prized today and destined to become even more valuable tomorrow.

The fun of collecting old kitchen items is that they can be readily found—in your own attic perhaps, at flea markets, garage sales, auctions and, yes, even in antique shops. Except in rare cases, they're not terribly expensive either, which makes kitchen collectibles an ideal gift for friends who like to cook. They'll appreciate your special thoughtfulness.

Photography/William Hazzard

Ruth Isgro's collection of kitchen antiques (left) in her Burlington Co., New Jersey home includes a water bench with spongeware, flow blue sugar bowl, butter-prints. Top shelf: wood spoons and toys, tin canisters, stoneware. On floor, a 24-inch flour canister, a coffee bin and grinder.

Kitchen collectibles in use (above). Container in foreground is a round wood spice box. Salt glaze crock with cobalt blue design, at left. Brown crock is a modern French import. Rolled cookies served from an ice cream mold. On wall, an iron cookie press, trivet, wood cookie molds (left one is old, others are new).

Sometimes called graniteware or agateware, enamelware was developed in the 1870s and was considered to be an elegant material. It was sheet iron, coated with bonded enamel and the first patterns were marbleized. It came in a range of colors; most sought after today is blue and white.

Enamelware found quick popularity in cooking utensils. It was lighter than iron and easier to clean. Soon it was used for soap dishes, buckets, cups, chamber pots, mixing bowls.

An even lighter-weight enamelware was enameled sheet tin. This found use in ladles, cups, tumblers, toilet articles, tureens, funnels. Almost all old enamelware found today will show chips and other signs of use; it was not as durable as its developers promised it to be.

## Enamelware

Large items on top shelf include coffee pot, bed pan, a red kettle for cooking and two kitchen pots. Small items are a drinking cup and toy mixing bowl, pot and measurer. Bottom shelf: milk kettle, child's potty, lunch pail with drinking cup top.

On back wall, a muffin pan, skewers, ice tongs, corndryer. On floor, mortar and pestle, three-legged pot, an unusual-shape fry pan, candy mold, letter holder, painted flat irons on holder, tea kettle. In center is a two-burner oil stove, about 20 inches tall, with small iron kettle on top.

## Ironware and Woodenware

Cast iron utensils, heavier than they are today, were a familiar sight in the 19th century kitchen. Often they were passed along to the next generation. Ironware was the most popular cookware of the period.

Some iron pots were enormous, with capacities up to 40 gallons and, in addition to cooking, these were used for candlemaking, yarn dyeing and for boiling clothes.

Iron, hand-forged or cast, was also used for such other items as corkscrews, choppers and mashers, egg boilers, pie crimpers, toasters and trivets.

Woodenware was popular for the hundred years preceding the 19th century. It was still in evidence in the second half of the 19th century, mainly in ladles, spoons and paddles. Wood was also often used as a component part; the washboard shown is just one example of this.

Photography / Al Reagan

From top left, a glass washboard with wood trim, a butter churn (center removed for display), and a two-piece canister set. Through the center: a child's washtub, square butter mold, a wool comber and a large water bucket. In the foreground: butter paddle, lemon squeezer, chopping bowl, butter print and a ladle, masher and paddle. One-piece pitcher is rare. Wooden cup at right is a noggin, which was used as a measurer.

Top shelf, an unusual tin coffeepot with off-center handle; miniature tea kettle; working tin snipe, used to lure birds; sugar shaker; cake decorator; small skater's lantern, to fit over candle; sander, used in letterwriting to dry ink; tin flatware with wood handles. Bottom shelf, candle holder, individual spice tin, spice box with small tins, boiler, strainer, coal bucket.

## Tinware and Wireware

Below (from top left), a large egg-gathering basket and one for storing eggs. In rear is a bird cage; in front of it, a child's ice cream chair and a wire mesh wastebasket. Two-pronged object, left foreground, is a Shaker pie lifter; on either side are rug beaters. Dome in center is a screen fly cover for food. Wool carder in center foreground.

**T**in vied with iron as the most popular cookware metal in the mid-19th century. Aluminum had not yet come on the scene; enamelware was available. Tin was a versatile and durable metal and was also considered safe. In fact, tin was used as a lining in copper and brass cooking utensils to guard against harmful chemical reactions from food acids. Today you'll find old tin items in wide variety. Most will have developed a dark patina, many will be dented. This photo suggests the widespread use of tin during the last century.

**M**ost wireware was made of tin-coated iron and much of it was imported, although the items themselves were made in the United States. Such things as whips, strainers, potato fryers, soap dishes and the like are still made today in essentially the same form. The strength and thickness of wire varies according to its use.

A wide open field for collectors. Items such as old soap packages and tin food or tobacco containers are bringing good prices today. Labels should be intact—better if wording is embossed on tin or glass. Start your search at home—in attic, cellar, on cupboard shelves.

## Grocery store items and Scales

Scales were standard equipment almost everywhere in the 19th century—in homes, stores, grist mills, pharmacies, the post office. You'll come upon them often in your search today, many selling for under $5.

The earliest scale was the steel-yard type—a long bar with a weight placed on one end. Other later types include the Challinor, which works on a spring; scoop scales, used in homes and stores alike to measure as well as weigh; platform scales, also based on the spring principle. Drug scales were capable of fine measurement. The open fish-type scale consisted of a pan attached by chains to a round-face spring scale. This type is still in use in many stores today, mainly for produce.

Egg scales, appearing around 1830, were used to measure and grade eggs, which at that time were sold by weight.

Scales that were in everyday use around the farm: far left, milk scale; next two are general purpose scales; fourth was possibly used for weighing tobacco; at right is a milk scale. Below is a yardarm scale used in butchering or weighing feeds. Board above it was used for meat drying and storage.

Below, from left, a pharmaceutical scale. Alongside, a 20th century postal scale. Second row, an early type kitchen scale; square platform is a 19th century postal scale. Rear, hanging scale was used to weigh produce; smaller scoop scale was a kitchen model.

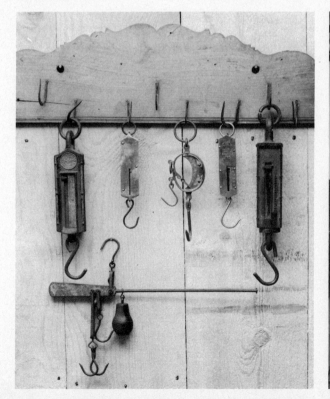

# Everyone could use another basket

**W**ith increasing appreciation for using natural materials, baskets have become highly desirable and cherished collectibles. It would be difficult to find anyone who wouldn't treasure one as a gift. Not only are baskets valued for their usefulness, but also for their craftsmanship—as examples of country or folk art.

From the time Moses was hidden in the "ark of the bullrushes. . . daubed with slime and with pitch," people throughout the world have made baskets from whatever materials were at hand. German farmers in Pennsylvania used rye straw; Indians in the Northeast used ash splints. Today, as in the past, Hopis use crushed leaves of yucca; the Mohawks use sweetgrass. If you want to find a basket made from corn husks, cane, bamboo, pine needles, willow, palm or cattail leaves, look in the regions where these plants grow.

### Basketmaking methods

The techniques for making baskets haven't changed too much over the years. Basically there are three: weaving, twining and coiling.

Woven baskets are made by weaving a horizontal weft over and under the vertical warp—in and out, the way you darn. Usually the warp and weft are made from the same material.

For the twining method, two or more wefts are twisted around each other as they are woven in and out of the vertical warps. Often the weft is of a flexible or pliable material and the finished basket looks like a needlepointed, crocheted or knitted container.

In the coiling method, a long continuous spiral of a flexible material is wound around and around into the desired shape, and the top coil is stitched to the previous row as it is worked. Because there are no spokes to weave in and out of, coiling is the easiest method to learn. (Directions for learning how to coil a bread basket follow.)

Wickerwork is sometimes labeled as a fourth method. Actually, some wicker baskets are woven, some are twined, some combine both methods. The material used is rattan or willow, which is round instead of flat.

### What to look for, where to buy

Everywhere you look—stores, craft shops, flea markets, country auctions, fairs—there is such a wide variety of types, sizes, designs and quality available that a choice may seem difficult at first. Do a little looking before you buy. Never miss an opportunity to visit museums. They can be treasure houses of information for the collector.

If you're a flea market addict, now is the time to buy old baskets. Dealers will tell you that prices have doubled in the past year. But with persistence, you can still get good values. Through experience you learn to recognize quality. When examining a basket, check the overall condition first, then inspect all the details carefully.

Check the weaving or stitching—is it evenly spaced? Are there missing or broken splints? Any loose ends? Any nails? If so, they should be hand forged in antique baskets. Baskets with metal bails, wire nails or staples, plastic trim are obviously newer varieties and not valuable as collectibles.

Baskets are fragile. Through use and natural drying conditions they become brittle. So what is the best way to preserve them? "About once a year, set them out in a gentle rain for a day," recommends Carroll Hopf, curator of the Pennsylvania Farm Museum of Landis Valley. "Or soak them in water for about half an hour. Either method not only restores some of the moisture but also washes off the accumulated dust."

Whether you just like the looks of baskets and use them decoratively, or are becoming an avid collector, the more you learn about them, the more interesting they become. Even more so if you share this interest with friends.

Photography/Bob Robinson    Room Settings/Gerald Belast and Staff, Bloomingdale's, Jenkintown

Baskets make great containers for plants. Large coiled basket on the floor holds a tree-sized dracaena marginata; smaller basket on the desk houses a container of grape ivy.

A long splat basket filled with books and dried eucalyptus leaves adds an imaginative touch to this mantel arrangement. For good composition use other collectibles—such as the Chinese box, stone statue, pottery pheasants and candlestick-lamp—in conjunction with baskets.

Bookshelves provide display space for baskets. French bakery shelf (above) holds Chinese baskets, woven with fine bamboo; round Colombian basket; splat basket for storing yarn; wicker basket filled with dried statice.

Coarsely woven Japanese basket (left) complements the feather arrangement.

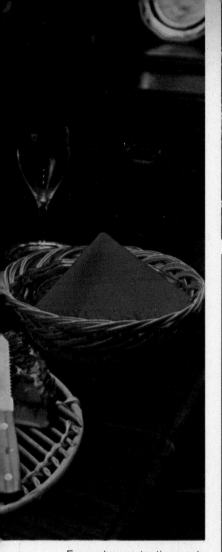

For a cheese-tasting party (above) use wicker bread baskets at each place and a handled basket in the center for an assortment of breads. Starflowers, bursting from a low basket, set the fall color theme.

African baskets hanging on the shutters (left) are coiled baskets—of red, brown and gold natural-dye colored fibers— accented with cowrie shells.

Baskets provide interesting shapes and designs for the wall. Winnowing baskets from Colombia (right) and an antique temple carving are arranged on a burnt-orange felt wall.

# Make a coiled bread basket

Photography/Bob Robinson

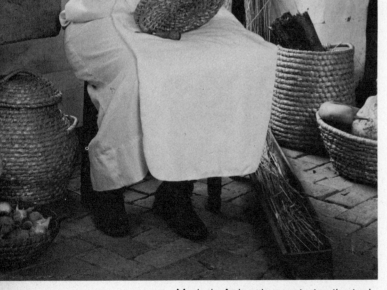

**O**nce you've made a basket, you begin to appreciate and become more sensitive to workmanship and quality in all baskets. But even more important is the joy in creating a useful object from everyday materials with almost no tools except your own two hands. That feeling of pride is something you'll share with other craftsmen each time you pick up one of their baskets.

Rye straw baskets made by Pennsylvania Dutch farmers are prized collector's items. Some of the best known examples come from the historic German Protestant settlement known as the Ephrata Cloister at Ephrata, Pennsylvania. Since its recent restoration, this Cloister has become an important stop on the Pennsylvania Trail of History.

If you make this stop on a summer Saturday, you can find Marjorie Auker (one of the guides in authentic costume) demonstrating the technique for making coiled baskets. But in case you can't make it to Ephrata in the very near future, Marjorie shares the techniques she has perfected for making a bread basket in this book.

Directions for making begin on page 139

Marjorie Auker demonstrates the technique for making a coiled fruit-drying tray at the restored Ephrata Cloister in Ephrata, Pa. She is surrounded by other baskets she has made.

# How to run a successful bazaar

Old-time bazaars, like so many other good things from the past, are being revived and are enjoying a new peak of popularity across the country. And as fund raisers, bazaars are without equal, especially around the holidays when money can best be raised for a worthy cause.

Reminiscent of the country fair, there are tables laden with the best cakes, cookies and jellies that local cooks have to offer. Colorful, handmade gifts and decorations fill the school hall or church meeting room, and a grand time is had by all. But behind the festive decorations and holiday gaiety, is a year of dedicated work. For those who organize the bazaar, it's a crucial merchandising event—the time when the value of their efforts is determined by the cash exchanged for their handiwork.

We took a close look from start to finish at two successful bazaars—a small one put on by beginners and an ambitious multi-group effort that has been successfully held each year since 1928. Many of the ideas from both of these bazaars are borrowable for your own event.

From a small beginning, the Women's Chapter of Daylesford Abbey in Pennsylvania raised $3600 after expenses. At the outset the Abbey contributed $200 for the purchase of materials for the bazaar items. From May through November some 42 volunteers met weekly and worked to provide distinctive handmade merchandise and gourmet foods. Successful bazaars do require that kind of effort. The bazaar was held on two days in December, two weeks apart.

In downtown Philadelphia, 38 separate service organizations joined together under the auspices of Emergency Aid of Pennsylvania for a giant bazaar in the ballroom of the Bellevue-Stratford Hotel. It was the 47th annual combined bazaar and is as much a part of the city's Yuletide as the arrival of Santa Claus. Each organization maintains its own booth. Emergency Aid also operates 10 booths to cover expenses and to raise funds of its own. This has the effect of 50 mini-bazaars. Emergency Aid financed the hotel location, and each organization kept its total proceeds, which ranged from $440 to $1800. The biggest money maker—Santa's Pack, a raffle offering about 50 prizes— brought in $6300!

The Emergency Aid United Bazaar might be a difficult plan to copy, but it does suggest that two or more groups in your area could add to the public's interest by planning a joint effort. It's a way to generate more publicity and draw a larger crowd. But singly or together, each group will have to structure its own bazaar. Here are some helpful guidelines we gleaned from the experience of the Daylesford group and the individual organizations in the Emergency Aid bazaar.

**Start lining up workers** eight to ten months in advance of the bazaar date. You might have to work at convincing some people that they have the skills you need; recruiting is a major step if your bazaar is to be successful. Divide your recruits into activity classifications—finance, sewing, cooking, crafts, special projects, publicity and arrangements. Appoint a chairman for each group to coordinate the work. It's essential that everyone be given something productive to do. In recruiting workers, utilize all of the available talent in your community—men, teenagers, senior citizens can all pitch in.

None of the groups we spoke with had to go outside its own ranks for volunteers but, if you do, a campaign letter can be very effective. Write to other groups in your area—members of the local PTA, church congregations, men's service clubs, youth groups, senior citizens clubs. You will find willing workers almost everywhere you look.

"Old Towne of Smithville," a historic whaling village now reconstructed and popular with tourists, inspired this picturesque booth at the Emergency Aid Bazaar.

**You'll need financing** for materials to get started, once you have gathered your workers. The old saying that you have to spend money to make money is true. Bazaar chairmen estimated $200 to $300 as a starting sum, and most said it came from the group's own treasury. If you're starting from scratch, an advance from the benefiting organization can usually be arranged. This, and the money individual workers may spend can be deducted from the final proceeds. The Daylesford group noted that its original $200 for materials was quickly spent and that members financed their own purchases through the summer and fall. They were reimbursed from final proceeds (although many declined to accept their total expenses).

Another way to get financing is to plan a pre-bazaar fund-raising event. To pay for the hotel location and its own ten booths, Emergency Aid holds a dinner dance in the spring and a pre-sale of bazaar items in the fall. Some groups start their bazaar financing by holding cake sales, car washes or whatever is popular in their area.

Have the finance chairman open a special checking account with your starting funds and make all payments out of this. When choosing the finance chairman, select someone who is good at handling money and can keep an accurate balance sheet. Remember that your primary objective is to raise money, not spend it.

**What to sell** is a big decision and this is one that has to be made early. People are always looking for new and unusual gift ideas—the same old tired repeats seen year after year at other bazaars just won't sell. So ask some of the creative people in your group to scout local stores or make a trip to the city to see what's new in the boutiques and craft shops. Christmas issues of women's magazines from previous years often can provide useful ideas. From the abundance of craft books on the market, you should be able to find enough good ideas to put together a wonderful potpourri of unique, saleable items.

When searching for possibilities, don't exclude purchased merchandise, food gifts, donations of the white elephant variety and plants.

Your resources and the special talents of your group are your guides for planning inventory. Sometimes new talents emerge; the crushed glass wreath and carpet picture were first tries by Daylesford workers—so was the patchwork map. Just remember to include items for men, women, young people and a variety of inexpensive items for children to give as gifts.

Divide your proposed stock into categories. The list of possibilities under each heading can be as long as your imagination suggests:

*Handmades:* The "tooth fairy" pillows shown here are novel ideas. Stuffed toys, tote bags, his and

134

her cook's aprons, shawls, and afghans are other good possibilities. Handmade candles are always appealing, as are decorative centerpieces. And don't forget a variety of Christmas wreaths and ornaments.

In foods, breads are irresistible, even those made from a mix—especially banana, pumpkin and nut breads. Cakes can be decoratively frosted for the holidays. Hors d'oeuvres, sauces and candies suggest their own packaging—in jars or arranged on attractive plates. Nuts, relishes and casseroles have a place on the foods table. Be sure to arrange for refrigeration if you sell cooked foods.

As a rule, useful items are better sellers than those merely decorative. However, the Daylesford group did well with decoupage plaques bearing a greeting card scene or verse. They were made by the husband of a volunteer and sold for $3.00. An Emergency Aid affiliate was successful in selling scene-pasted pins made of old eye glass lenses. These were made by hospitalized children and sold for 50¢ each.

If you live in or near a big city you'll find wholesale suppliers for the materials you'll need for craft and handmade items. Frequently, a retail art or craft shop will give you a discount on bulk purchases, but don't count on it. Most of the chairmen told us it's just as economical, and convenient, to order supplies by mail. Some good sources: Lee Wards (Elgin, Illinois 60120), The Handcrafters (Waupun, Wisconsin 53963), Home-Sew, Inc. (Bethlehem, Pa. 18018). Write for catalogs.

*Purchased merchandise:* The number one rule in purchasing: Buy in quantity. A local store might provide merchandise on a consignment basis enabling you to return the unsold items. Or mail order houses may give bulk discounts. Even if you have to buy outright, store the leftovers to sell later or even at next year's bazaar. The important thing is choosing unusual and appealing items of good design, preferably not too available in local stores.

Jewelry, novel housewares, accessories for the bath, items for purse and car, glassware and candle holders are good possibilities listed in many mail order catalogs. Miles Kimball (41 W. 8th Avenue, Oshkosh, Wisconsin 54901) or Sunset House (202 Sunset Building, Beverly Hills, California 90215) or Downs (1014 Davis Street, Evanston, Illinois 60204) offer a world of inspiration in their catalogs. And it's worth asking for a bulk discount. One of the Emergency Aid organizations had great success with 350 jewelry items and 120 fruit cakes, which were all purchased. They earned a quantity discount.

If the beneficiary of your bazaar is a religious, charitable or other non-profit organization, it probably has a tax-exempt number. Use this number when ordering merchandise or supplies—it will

For pine cone wreath, wire large cones to outer edge of a heavy wire circle. Add more cones and berries inward. Cut tops off Scotch pine cones; wire to form inner outline. Spray white.
Shadow box for angel is a plastic carton top. Secure angel with floral clay and add cotton for cloud effect. Bottom wreath uses pieces of broken glass.

Photography/Al Reagan

For wire basket, buy one yard of "hardware cloth" at hardware store. Comes in 36" width. Cut into four 18" squares (enough for 4 baskets). Pull diagonally opposite corners together and tie with wire. Cut enough 1½" wide velvet ribbon to cover all edges. Line ribbon with pressure sensitized (rug) tape. Apply to edges of hardware cloth. Wire on velvet bow at top.

Tooth fairy pillows are two-size knife edge type with ruffles added. Pocket in small one is more like a bound buttonhole. House and pocket on large one (15 × 15") are appliques, with details outlined in embroidery floss.

stretch your buying power. And, whether dealing with a retailer or mail order house, always mention your bazaar, the benefiting organization, and ask for any possible discount.

*Donations:* White elephants, usually books and attic treasures, can be collected from virtually everybody within reach, including bazaar workers. Remember, white elephant donations are pure profit.

*Plants:* Home-grown Christmas greens, as well as small potted plants, make wonderful bazaar items now that plants are "big." It isn't absolutely necessary to go into fancy pots, but colorful displays and unusual plant hangers do help sales.

**Hold regular workshops,** although it's obvious that most handwork will be made at home. They're fun, result in good fellowship and produce new ideas—the Humpty Dumpty music plaque is a good example. Then keep everybody working on schedule. One tip: Get to work immediately upon arrival; you can chat while you work.

Members of the group who are not especially talented at putting things together can often do preparatory steps for others—such as fringing burlap for wreaths, crushing glass for plaques, cutting fabrics, painting or whatever.

How many of each item to make depends on the time it takes to complete one. A rule of thumb might be a dozen of each in the case of dolls, stuffed animals or pillows. For Christmas tree ornaments, however, you could make as many as ten dozen or more. But always try to anticipate your sales.

The food table is always popular; so make enough breads, cookies, cakes and candies to meet the demand. The Daylesford group packaged fudge in attractive reusable containers—baskets, planters and such—and did a rushing business.

**Fair, profitable prices** for your merchandise are not always easy to arrive at. You won't recoup the value of labor on handmade or food items, but add 100% above the cost of materials and a nominal sum for labor. For purchased merchandise add about 40% to cost, but stay within the price range of your public. Prices on bought merchandise should not be above the cost of comparable items in a store.

Make prices plainly visible. Use small self-stick labels and write figures clearly. If some items prove to be overpriced consider a final-hour clearance sale at lower prices. Decide in advance the reduced price and assign someone to mark the labels. Don't undersell, however. Items that are left behind might sell quickly at the next meeting of your own group. Or you can always make them part of next year's beginnings.

Wall hanging uses carpet scraps. Mount background fabric on 16 × 19″ Cellutex. Glue design pieces to background; outline details with glued-on wool yarn.

To make apple-head, soak firm apple for two minutes in water. Carve exaggerated features with a sharp knife. Insert cloves for eyes. Store in a dry place 2-3 weeks, molding features during this time. For body, bend an 18″ wire in half like a hairpin. Draw through apple until round end of wire is at stem end of apple. For arms, attach a second piece of 18″ wire to first wire an inch below head. Wrap scrap fabric around body and limbs. Whip-stitch in place. Dress by choice.

Mushroom basket has a Styrofoam base, fitted snuggly. Cover artificial mushrooms with gingham, add wire to stems to insert into Styrofoam. Arrange greens to fill space and cover Styrofoam.

**Storage will present problems** of expense and security, as your merchandise accumulates. Ask committee chairmen to house items made or ordered by their groups and to take responsibility for delivering them to the bazaar.

**A raffle or two** can really swell your coffers, if your community has no objection. Merchandise is not the only money maker to consider. The Daylesford group raffled a patchwork map of the United States, made by a member of the crafts group, and cleared $90. For the second day they offered another patchwork map plus a $50 money tree and a knit stole and cleared $175.

The success of Emergency Aid's Santa's Pack raffle was outstanding. All prizes—about 50—were donated by local merchants and individuals. The public bought tickets outside the bazaar ballroom near the display of prizes. This raffle was the single most profitable feature of the entire bazaar, clearing $6300. Most of the participating organizations also held raffles at their respective booths.

Another extra feature to consider is a snack bar or meal service. Daylesford anticipated and received largely an adult crowd. They sold coffee and Danish (50¢) in the morning and served sherry (50¢) in the afternoon—both snack items were popular. Emergency Aid, through the hotel facilities, served a buffet luncheon, but expressed disappointment because it had to be priced so high—$6.00.

They favor the snack bar idea used previously.

Emergency Aid also did what others fear to try—they charged $1.00 admission to the bazaar itself. Remember that this bazaar offered 50 booths for browsing and attracted a crowd of downtown business people during the two days. However, an admission fee can inhibit attendance in a smaller location.

**The publicity committee** should go into action about two months before bazaar date with press releases to the club editor or the women's editor of each newspaper in your area—even in neighboring towns. This should be typewritten double-spaced on a single sheet of paper, and include date, time and location of the bazaar. The sender should write her name and telephone number in the upper right-hand corner so the editor can contact her, if necessary, for more information. It's also a good idea to write a short note to the editor inviting photo coverage of one of your workshop sessions.

Most radio stations are happy to mention community events. Send your information about two weeks in advance and address it to the program director.

Use posters to spread your message, too. If there's a sign shop in town you can have them made professionally. If not, enlist the help of talented amateurs and students. See that the posters are placed

Patchwork map makes a significant wall hanging for home or club room. Covers continental United States and requires 48 pieces of small-print cotton fabrics, plus paisley print for the Great Lakes. Trace map on tracing paper, eliminating unnecessary contour complications. Make second tracing. Transfer outline of tracing to 15 × 20″ art cardboard. Use other tracing to maneuver fabric placements. Make an index card for each state and glue on fabric for that state. With tracing face down on back of index card, trace state and cut through fabric with X-acto knife. Mount fabric covered pieces on map using Mod Podge glue. Refine state edges with X-acto knife. Frame with 2½″ mat in color of choice; cover with non-glare glass.

in as many public spots as possible—the library, store windows, church, the school or location where the bazaar will be held.

**The arrangement committee** can search out a site for your bazaar if it's necessary. They will also see to the setting up of selling tables and the general decor of the room. Bright table coverings can be fashioned from inexpensive materials, or even crepe paper. Be sure to provide access for people entering and leaving the room and arrange tables for an orderly flow of traffic. Make aisles as wide as possible to accommodate browsers. Background music adds to festivity, so borrow a record player or tape deck but keep it *background* music.

Duration of the bazaar should also be decided by the arrangement committee. Both groups agreed that two days were better than one but, of course, this varies locally.

**When bazaar day arrives,** assign committee workers to sell at their own tables and recruit extra help as necessary. Men and teenagers come in handy. Each chairman should see that a supply of change is on hand at the tables—about $20. This sum is usually withdrawn from the treasury. A finance committee member should be seated in an accessible place to take checks.

Although not absolutely necessary, it's a nice touch to provide wrappings of some kind for the items you're selling, especially foods. Committee chairmen should arrange this with their groups.

Time flies once a bazaar gets underway. You won't know how much you've made until all expenses have been deducted. But you will know that all the preparation time was needed and begin to feel that the next year you should start earlier. Experience is valuable and next year's bazaar will be better for it.

# Instructions

## Basket Instructions

### Rye Straw Bread Basket

**Materials**

- Rye straw: If you know a farmer who grows rye, you're in luck. Ask if you can cut some when it's ripe. Otherwise, you'll need to grow a few rows of your own. (Oat and wheat straw are shorter than rye and are not as durable. So rye is your best bet.) At Ephrata Cloister, they grow two varieties of rye: Tetra-Petkus—coarse stemmed—and Balbo—a fine-textured variety. Sow the seed (order from your local seed dealer) in the fall, harvest when ripe—usually during June, depending on the region. Don't use green straw—it shrinks as it dries and distorts the basket, or makes the weave too loose.

- Stitching material: ¼″ flat reed. Unlike caning, this material is flat on both sides. You can buy flat reed wherever caning supplies are sold (see a list of suppliers at the end of these instructions). It's usually priced by the 1-lb. bundle—enough for four or five baskets.

- Punching tool: Anything with a blunt end for punching an opening in the straw to make way for the reed stitching will do. Marjorie Auker uses a short, 6″ screwdriver with a ¼″ blade.

- Shears: Use a heavy pair that will cut the reed and trim the straw.

**1.** Gather a large handful of straw. Cut off seed heads and husk each straw to reveal the clean, golden sheen.

**2.** Soak the straw in lukewarm water for at least an hour. Marjorie Auker uses a soaking trough constructed from a 6′ piece of gutter spout. Although you can soak the straw in the bathtub, it's a pretty messy proposition, and you may clog the drain. (Note: Don't soak the reed. Wet reed has too much resistance for sewing.)

**3.** You are now ready to begin your pinwheel that starts the base (bottom) of the basket. This is the most difficult part. Once you master it, making the rest of the basket is easy. Select the finest texture straw you can—it's easier to control—for the beginning coil. Gather a handful of straw about ½″ in diameter. (When making the basket try to maintain this ½″ diameter so that all the coils will be the same size. Whenever you think the diameter of the straw is getting smaller, pick up more stems from the soaking batch and insert them, one at a time, into the center of the straw and twist them.)

**4.** Hold the straw in your left hand. Pick up a length of reed in your right hand. Position end of reed in front of straw about 4 or 5″ from the end of the straw. Begin wrapping reed, working from right to left, over the top of straw. Bring reed around straw and up from the bottom toward you and over again the second time forming an X as shown in Fig. 1. Wrap again over top of straw, always working right to left, to secure end of reed. (Note: Always pull the entire length of reed between your forefinger and thumb to keep it from tangling. This continued friction will make your fingers sore so you may want to wear a pliable glove.)

**5.** Now that the straw is fastened together with the reed, trim the 4 or 5″ of straw that you left at the end to about 1½″. With your right thumb, coax the 1½″ straw ends (takes time and persistence) into making a U-turn so that the straw doubles on itself (Fig. 2). Hold straw together for neat work. Hold straw with left hand, keeping reed in position with left thumb.

**6.** Now you are ready to make the center core. Bring reed toward you and over top away from you. Complete wrap by bringing reed through the center of the straw U (Fig. 3). Now you have the correct start for wrapping reed around the straw. You will always be pulling the reed through the hole in the straw U from the back, up through the bottom, and over the top.

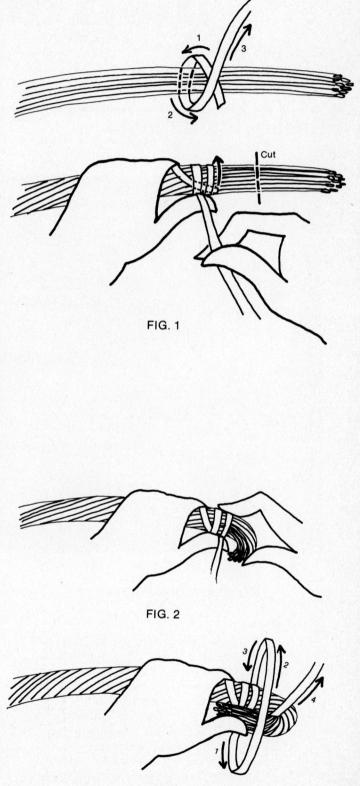

FIG. 1

FIG. 2

FIG. 3

**7.** Now the center core is finished, and you're ready to start the pinwheel itself. With the left hand, start twisting the straw toward you (about half a turn); at the same time, turn the straw to make the coil (Fig. 4). You will be twisting the straw as you form the coils for the entire basket—the twist is what gives the basket its firmness.

FIG. 4

**8.** As you form the coil, thread the reed over it away from you toward the back, then up from the bottom and through the center hole. Continue in this way: twisting the straw, turning the coil, and weaving the reed until you have a complete pinwheel (Fig. 5). It takes about 7 to 9 wraps to make this first pinwheel. The tighter you can hold the straw as you weave, the firmer the center pinwheel will be. After the pinwheel has been completed, you no longer go through the center hole for stitching.

FIG. 5

**9.** You are now ready to weave the bottom of the basket. With the screwdriver, punch an opening in the straw just below the first stitch of the pinwheel—and out on the top on the other side of the stitch (Fig. 6). Thread the reed through the punched hole and wrap it around the straw coil to complete the stitch. For each new stitch, punch a hole between two stitches in the first coil and continue twisting, coiling, threading the reed and wrapping it. Note: When you come to the end of a piece of reed, push it back through the coil, around the previous stitch and forward toward you again (Fig. 7). Clip off the end of the reed close to the coil, and it will disappear into the straw.

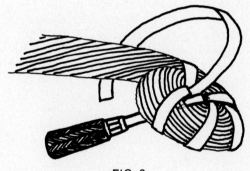

FIG. 6

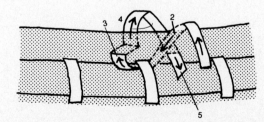

FIG. 7

**10.** To start the new reed (Fig. 8), push the starting end in at the same place the previous piece ended. Push this end into the center of the straw coil; it will never show. Then continue weaving.

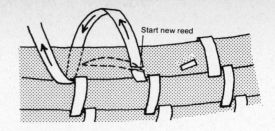

FIG. 8

**11.** As the diameter of your basket gets larger, the stitches will get farther and farther apart. To keep the stitches 1 to 1½″ apart, it may be necessary to insert an extra stitch now and then between the two stitches in the previous row (Fig. 9).

**12.** When you have worked the bottom of the basket to the desired diameter (ours is 5″, but you can make it larger) you are ready to start the upturned sides. Up until this point you have been weaving the coils in a flat plane, now you must lift them about ⅛″ as you work around the circumference of the base. This means that you will punch your opening weave through the straw coil a little higher each time.

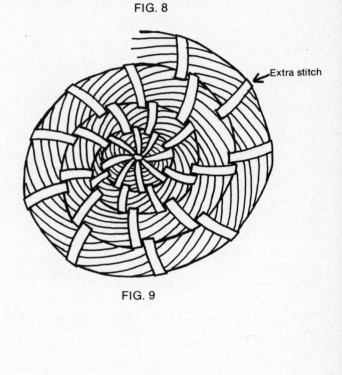

FIG. 9

**13.** To finish the top of the basket, stop adding straw when the basket is the desired height. (The one we show was ended after 8 coils.) Let the straw dwindle down to nothing on the last row. Double up on the reed stitches for the final row to give the rim extra sturdiness. To end the reed, weave it back and forth through the straw coil just once (end on inside of basket), then clip off the exposed end close to the coil.

**14.** After completing basket, use shears to clip stray pieces of straw that may be sticking out all over.

**Suppliers**

You can buy ¼″ flat reed wherever chair caning supplies are sold. Or order a 1-lb. hank (approximately 370′) from one of the following suppliers. Write them for prices.

Boin Arts & Crafts Company
87 Morris Street
Morristown, New Jersey 07960

H. H. Perkins Co.
10 South Bradley Road
Woodbridge, Connecticut 06525

Cane and Basket Supply Co.
1283 South Cochran Avenue
Los Angeles, California 90019

Naturalcraft
2199 Bancroft Way
Berkeley, California 94704

# Gifts to Sew Instructions

### Ruffled Hostess Apron

**Materials**

- 3⅓ yds. cotton fabric, 45″ wide
- 6 yds. wide rickrack
- Thread

**Directions**

**1.** Cut apron pieces, per the dimensions in Fig. 1. (Note: Finished apron is 33″ from waist to hem in front. You may lengthen or shorten apron by adjusting length of skirt piece. Finished waistband is 24″ long. It should not overlap in back; there should be a space of 2″, or more, so that ties can be made easily into a bow. Add or subtract to waistband if necessary for a better fit.) To get true bias for ruffles, check exact width of your fabric, then measure down that amount to block off a perfect square. Draw a diagonal line connecting opposite corners; measure ruffles from the diagonal lines. Follow dimensions in Fig. 1 to shape bottom curve of skirt. (Note: You have enough fabric left to cut two hot-pad mitts.) Seam allowances are ½″ unless otherwise stated.

**2.** For skirt ruffle, join all the 7″-wide sections to form one continuous strip. Turn a narrow hem lengthwise along one side. Stitch and press. Ruffle is tapered at each end. To do this, work on the side that is not hemmed. Measure in 36″ from each end; mark. Draw a straight line from this mark, across strip to corner on hemmed side. Cut along this line. Gather full length of strip along unhemmed edge.

**3.** Position ruffle on skirt. Ruffle begins at top edge, goes down one side, across bottom, up the opposite side. Divide ruffle so that gathers will be even; pin in place. Stitch and press.

**4.** To make ties, fold each tie in half lengthwise, wrong side out. Stitch across one end and down the length. Turn to right side. Press.

**5.** Gather top of skirt to fit waistband; make gathers ½″ from raw edge.

**6.** At each narrow end of waistband, turn raw edge ½″ to wrong side; press. Place right side of waistband (lengthwise) against wrong side of skirt top. Pin and stitch along line of gathers on skirt. Press waistband up.

**7.** Fold waistband to right side. Turn raw edge under and pin along line of gathers. Position ties; fit one tie to each end of waistband by making a pleat in the tie. To stitch waistband to skirt, begin

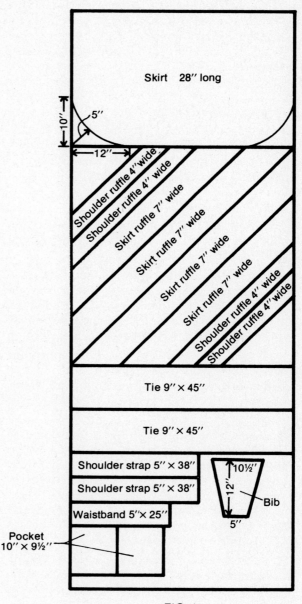

**FIG. 1**

at one end. Topstitch across the end to hold tie, turn and stitch along front, turn and stitch across opposite end.

**8.** Make shoulder ruffles, using the 4″-wide bias strips. For one ruffle, take one long and one short strip (see Fig. 1) and stitch them together. Join remaining two strips. Next, turn a narrow hem lengthwise along one side of each strip. Stitch and press. Ruffles should be tapered at each end. To do this, handle one strip at a time and work on the side that is not hemmed. Measure in 10″ from each end and mark. Draw a straight line from this mark across strip to corner on hemmed side; cut along this line. Gather ruffle along the unhemmed edge.

**9.** Add shoulder ruffles to straps. First, fold straps in half lengthwise, wrong sides together; press. Next, turn raw edges ½" to wrong side; press. Arrange the two straps parallel with folded edges next to each other; ruffles will be attached along open edges of straps to give you a right and left shoulder ruffle. On each strap, measure up 1" from one end (this will be the front); mark. From this point, mark off an additional 24"; ruffles will be inserted between these two marks.

**10.** Position ruffles between the marks on the straps. Slip raw edge of each ruffle between folded edges of strap. Pin and topstitch entire length of strap along the edge, catching ruffle in place. (Note: Be sure you make a right and a left strap, with ruffle beginning 1" from front edge.)

**11.** Work with bib section. Turn top edge 1½" to wrong side; press. Then turn the raw edge under and stitch.

**12.** Position straps with ruffles on top of bib; line up outside edge of each strap with outside edge of bib. Let end of ruffles meet bottom of bib (straps will be at an angle); pin in place and stitch along both edges of straps, securing them to bib.

**13.** Position bib with straps at front of apron. Match center of bib with center of waistband. Let waistband overlap bib by 1½". Pin in place. Stitch along top edge of waistband, catching bib as you go.

**14.** Secure loose ends of straps to waistband at back. (Note: Straps do not cross in back.) Try on apron to get exact fit (it will be about 32" from front of strap to back); mark. Stitch straps in place. Or make a buttonhole at this mark. Then, make two more buttonholes—one 1" above, and one 1" below the first buttonhole. Sew buttons to ends of waistband on the inside.

**15.** Add rickrack for trim. First, pin rickrack along ruffles on skirt; stitch. Next, stitch rickrack along center of shoulder straps, then along center of waistband.

## Hot-Pad Mitts

### Materials

- ⅓ yd. fabric, 45" wide, for outside
- ⅓ yd. fabric, 45" wide, for lining of one layer. (Note: If terry cloth or other lining fabric is not thick enough to give protection, use two or more layers.)
- 3 yds. double fold bias tape
- Thread

**Directions**

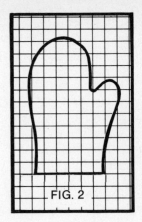

FIG. 2

**1.** Enlarge pattern in Fig. 2, using a 1" square for each square shown on the grid.

**2.** For each mitt, cut a front and a back from outside fabric.

**3.** For each mitt, cut a front and a back from lining fabric.

**4.** If you use several layers of lining, stack layers for front and stitch along the edge to hold them together. Repeat for back layers.

**5.** Work with front section. Place outside fabric over lining. Pin in place, and stitch along the top edge, catching all layers. Cover top edge with bias tape and stitch. (Note: Use a zigzag stitch if your machine has one; this catches both sides of tape in one operation.)

**6.** Repeat Step 5 for back section.

**7.** Join mitt front to mitt back. Leave top edge open; pin along curved edges. Stitch close to the edge, catching all layers of fabric. Trim close to stitching and grade the raw edges (hold scissors at an angle to taper fabric layers.)

**8.** Cover the raw edges with folded bias tape. Begin at the top edge on the thumb side; stitch around mitt, ending at the top edge on the other side. Leave an extra 3½" length of tape when you cut it; this will form a loop for hanging the mitt. Stitch tape to close it; then turn it to the inside of the mitt and catch end to the top edge.

## Landscape Apron

### Materials

- ½ yd. firm cotton fabric, 36" or 45" wide, for background of apron
- ½ yd. printed cotton fabric, 36" or 45" wide, for border
- ⅓ yd. cotton, 36" or 45" wide, in contrasting color for waistband
- Small pieces of cotton fabric in various colors for appliques
- Small pieces of lightweight iron-on interfacing (to back appliques)
- Embroidery floss in assorted colors
- Thread

## Directions

1. Enlarge pattern in Fig. 3, using a 1″ square for each square on the grid. Copy details on pattern to show design placement. Make separate patterns for appliques.

2. From background fabric, cut the apron (22″ wide, 16½″ long). Mark position of darts.

3. Stitch in the two darts at waistline. Press darts toward center of apron.

4. Cut fabric for border. First, cut a rectangle 22″ wide and 16½″ long, the exact size of the background piece. Next, measure in 4″ along each side, and measure up 4″ along bottom edge. Mark, and cut out center section, leaving a 4″ border along the two sides and the bottom.

5. Work with border. Along the sides and bottom edges, turn fabric ½″ to wrong side (clip inside corners to allow fabric to turn under). Press. (Note: Both inside and outside edges of border should be turned under.)

6. On apron, along the sides and bottom edge, turn fabric ½″ to right side; press.

7. Position border on top of background fabric, lining up bottom and side edges (raw edges will be sandwiched between the layers). Pin and topstitch along the outside edge. Leave inside edge of border turned under, but do not stitch until later.

8. For appliques, use patterns to cut design from iron-on interfacing, adhesive side up. Iron these pieces to the wrong side of the applique fabric; cut fabric, allowing ¼″ seam allowances all around the design.

9. Position applique pieces. Where a large piece meets the apron border, let it extend under the border. For other pieces, turn raw edges under ¼″ and sew to background fabric by hand.

10. Topstitch inside edge of border to apron.

11. To outline the applique pieces, chain stitch around them with embroidery floss. Use a chain stitch also for tree trunks, birds, the caterpillar, and for the extra rows of color on the ground areas.

12. Make waistband. Cut one strip 3″ wide and 19″ long; this is the center section. Cut two strips 3″ wide and 36″ long; these are the ties. Join the three sections, right sides together to make one long strip; position the center section between the two ties.

13. To add waistband to apron, work first with the band. On one long edge, turn fabric ½″ to wrong side; press. Find lengthwise center of band; mark. Find center of apron along top edge; mark. Place right side of waistband against wrong side of apron, matching center marks. Pin band to apron; stitch, using a ½″ seam allowance.

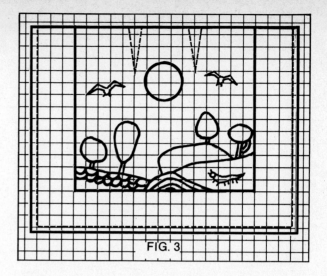

FIG. 3

14. Press waistband up. Fold band to right side of apron. Turn free edge (along length of band) ½″ to wrong side and pin to apron front, just overlapping first stitching line. Continue working along the ties; turn raw edges ½″ to wrong side and line up turned edges of ties. Also, turn ends of ties in ½″ and pin. Begin stitching at end of one tie. Stitch across end; turn and stitch along the length of the tie, the waistband, and the other tie.

## Patchwork Tie

Front of tie has four graduated squares. These can be made of one fabric, or they can be a patchwork of two—or four—different fabrics. All seam allowances are ¼″ unless otherwise noted.

### Materials

- ½ yd. fabric for background, 45″ wide
- Small pieces of fabric for squares
- ⅓ yd. lightweight fabric for lining
- ⅔ yd. special tie interfacing, 25″ wide (Note: This is enough to cut interfacings for two ties.)
- Thread

### Directions

1. Enlarge patterns in Fig. 4, and label them. Use a 1″ square for each square shown on the grid. (Note: On all patterns, copy center lines and arrows to indicate straight grain of fabric. Dotted lines on main patterns (Fig. 4-A, 4-B, 4-C) indicate seam allowances. Pattern Fig. 4-A is diagrammed to show position of squares when assembled.)

2. Save pattern Fig. 4-A to use later. Place patterns Fig. 4-B and 4-C on background fabric, but do not cut. Refer to Fig. 5. Follow measurements on non-shaded areas, and mark these strips on background fabric; follow arrows for straight

grain of fabric. Rearrange if necessary, so that you get all seven strips and patterns Fig. 4-B and 4-C on the fabric. Cut fabric.

**3.** From lining fabric, cut Fig. 4-D and 4-E; set these aside.

**4.** From interfacing fabric, cut patterns Fig. 4-F and 4-G; set these aside.

**5.** *If squares will be of one fabric,* refer to Fig. 5. Shaded areas give you the size for each square (these include ¼″ seam allowances). Measurements vary only slightly, so be accurate. Cut squares from fabric, then skip to Step 9.

**6.** *If squares will be patchwork,* refer to Fig. 7; this shows arrangement of patches. Then, refer to Fig. 6 which gives measurements for triangle patterns (these include ¼″ seam allowances). Enlarge triangle patterns. Measurements vary only a small amount, so be accurate. Mark arrows to indicate straight grain of fabric.

**7.** Place triangles on fabric, trace around them and cut. If you are using four different fabrics, cut one triangle of each size from each fabric. If you are using two different fabrics for the squares, cut two triangles of each size from each fabric.

**8.** Arrange patches for color; use Fig. 7 as a guide. Stitch triangles together; press seams open.

**9.** To join squares to background fabric, refer to Fig. 5. Arrange squares in position with strips of background fabric, already cut. Join squares to strips, working across diagram; press seams open. Next, join the long strips, working up the diagram (tips of the squares will touch); press seams open.

**10.** Place enlarged pattern Fig. 4-A on top of section you have just stitched. Line up top edges and bottom edges; have center line running diagonally through the squares. Pin in place; trim away excess background fabric.

**11.** Stitch section Fig. 4-A to section Fig. 4-B, right sides together; press seam open.

**12.** Stitch section Fig. 4-B to section Fig. 4-C, right sides together; press seam open.

**13.** Prepare lining sections Fig. 4-D and 4-E. Trim 1/16″ from sides and bottom edges; this avoids excess fullness when tie is finished.

**14.** Pin lining sections in place, right sides together. Section Fig. 4-D lines large end of tie (Fig. 4-A); section Fig. 4-E lines small end of tie. Stitch; turn to right side. Press.

**15.** Join the two sections of interfacing, Fig. 4-F and 4-G, by overlapping at seam lines. Stitch; trim close to stitching line.

**16.** Lay tie flat, right side down; have large end to your right. Place interfacing on top of tie, large end to the right. Match neck seams; center of interfacing should line up with center of tie. Pin in place. By hand, lightly catch interfacing to neck

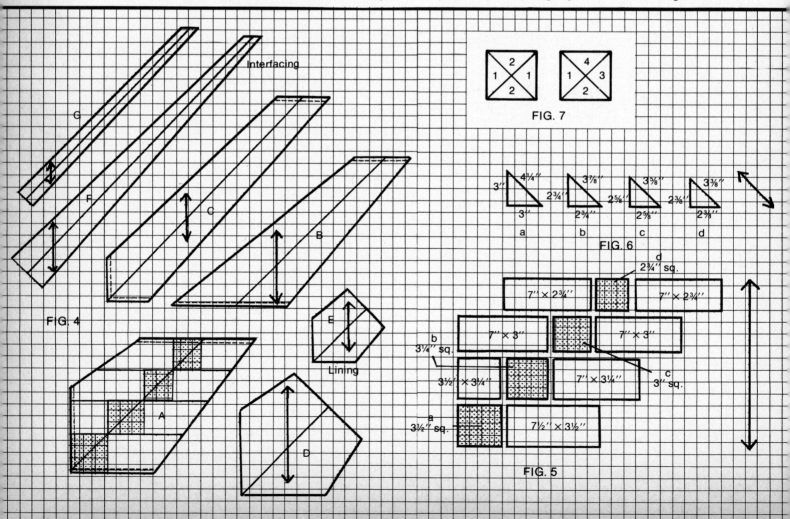

FIG. 7

FIG. 6

FIG. 4

FIG. 5

Interfacing

Lining

seam of tie and to lining at both ends.

**17.** Fold top edge of tie down over interfacing. (Note: Fold will run along outside edges of squares in section Fig. 4-A. For rest of tie, use interfacing as a guide for folding; raw edge of first turn will be about ⅜″ beyond center line.) Pin in place. At top of lining at each end, clip tie fabric just to seam line; this lets the fabric lie flat. With long hand stitches, catch raw edge of tie to interfacing; do not catch front of tie in these stitches.

**18.** Fold up lower edge of tie, using edges of squares as your guide, and overlapping first turn. Fold raw edge under ¼″. Catch in place with small hand stitches; leave 2½″ open at each end of tie.

**19.** Press tie lightly along folded edges; do not press flat.

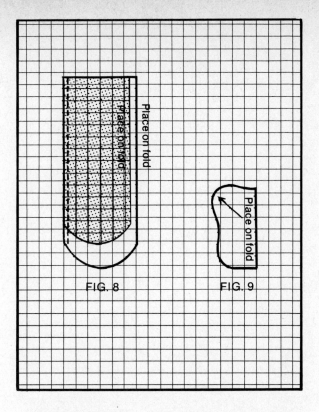

FIG. 8    FIG. 9

## Shoe Mitts

### Materials

- ½ yd. stretchy knit (Note: 60″-wide fabric is enough for two pairs of mitts.)
- Thread
- 1 yd. narrow (¼″ or less) ribbon or braid for drawstrings

### Directions

**1.** Enlarge pattern in Fig. 8, using a 1″ square for each square on the grid. Small pattern is for woman's shoe; large pattern is for man's shoe.

**2.** Place pattern on a fold of fabric and cut. Fold fabric again and cut another mitt.

**3.** For each mitt, open fabric and stitch along the top edge. (Note: For all stitching, use a zigzag stitch if your machine has one. Otherwise, stretch the fabric as you stitch it.)

**4.** Fold the mitt, right sides together. Using a ¼″ seam allowance, stitch down the side and across the curved bottom.

**5.** Turn the top edge ½″ to the wrong side. Stitch along raw edge to make a tunnel, leaving a small opening to insert the drawstring.

**6.** Cut ribbon or braid into two sections, ½ yd. each. Insert one length in each tunnel; knot the ends to prevent fraying.

## Eyeglass Case

### Materials

- Firm fabric, 8″ square, for outside
- Soft fabric, 8″ square, for lining
- Firm interfacing, 8″ square (Note: You may

want to use two sections of interfacing to give more firmness.)
- ½ yd. fold-over woven braid
- Thread

### Directions

**1.** Enlarge pattern in Fig. 9, using a 1″ square for each square shown on the grid. This gives you half the pattern.

**2.** To get a whole pattern, place the half pattern on a folded piece of paper (straight edge along fold); trace and cut. Open the pattern. Add arrow marks.

**3.** Use whole pattern, and cut one outside, one lining and one or two interfacings.

**4.** Stack fabric. On bottom, put outside fabric, right side down. Next, add interfacing. On top, place lining, right side up. Baste down center to hold layers in place.

**5.** Fold layers down center (layers will not be even at edges). Baste along middle of each side; trim edges to make them even. Now, handle layers as one fabric.

**6.** Apply braid by hand or machine (zigzag stitch is good). Begin at arrow mark on one side of case and work across top of case; fold braid over raw edges of case. When you come to arrow mark on other side, fold braid to enclose raw edges on both sides of case; be sure to cover cut edge of braid where you began. Continue down the side and across the bottom.

## Placemats, Table Runner

Directions are for making 6 patchwork placemats (lined), 6 napkins, and a table runner with 3 patchwork blocks at center.

### Materials

- 2 yds. cotton fabric, 45″ wide (first color)
- 2 yds. cotton fabric, 45″ wide (second color)
- 2½ yds. cotton fabric, 45″ wide (third color). Additional ½ yard is for runner end pieces. (Note: Finished runner is 82″ long and fits a 64″-long table. You can adjust length of runner by altering length of end pieces.)
- Thread

### Directions

**1.** Enlarge patterns for triangles a, b, c and d in Fig. 10. Cut the patterns from cardboard so that you can trace around them; patterns include ¼″ seam allowances. Draw in arrows indicating straight grain of fabric. (Note: Triangles in Fig. 10-a and 10-c are the same size, but are placed on fabric differently. You may cut one triangle, then mark one side for Fig. 10-a and the opposite side for Fig. 10-c).

**2.** Follow layout in Fig. 11 for sizes and placement of pieces. Cut all pieces shown from each of the three colors of fabric. (Exception: Cut end pieces for runner only from third color.)

**3.** Follow Fig. 12 for assembling placemats. Use ¼″ seam allowances. For each placemat, use a center square and end pieces of the same color; use triangles of the remaining two colors. (Note: You may wish to arrange pieces for all placemats before you begin to stitch.)

**4.** To assemble one placemat, join two triangles (Fig. 10-a) of different colors along the short length. Stitch with right sides together; press seam open. Repeat with three other pairs of triangles. You now have four larger triangles.

**5.** Stitch the larger triangles to the center square, right sides together. Press seams open.

**6.** Add the end pieces to the block, right sides together. Press seams open.

**7.** Topstitch along all seams to hold them flat; use a zigzag stitch if your machine has one.

**8.** To add lining, position placemat on top of lining, right sides together. Stitch together with ¼″ seam allowances, leaving an opening for turning. Turn to right side. Press. Close opening with hand stitches. Topstitch along all edges; use zigzag stitch if your machine has one.

**9.** Repeat Steps 3 through 8 to assemble five more placemats.

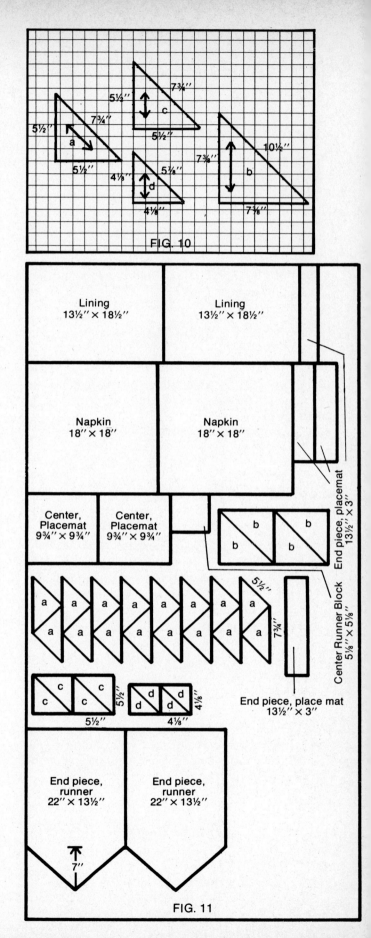

FIG. 10

FIG. 11

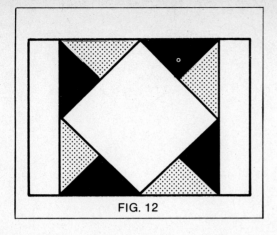

FIG. 12

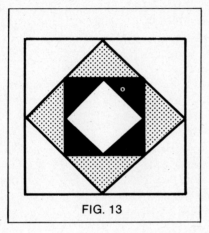

FIG. 13

## Man's Apron

### Materials

- 1 yd. fabric, 45″ wide
- 5 yd. fold-over woven braid
- Thread

### Directions

**1.** Enlarge pattern in Fig. 17, using a 1″ square for each square shown on the grid. This gives you half the pattern. Mark pocket placement on pattern.

**2.** Fold fabric lengthwise, turning in one edge 18″ (fold will not be in center of fabric). Place long side of pattern along fold, with bottom edge of pattern near bottom edge of fabric. Pin, and cut fabric. From remaining fabric, cut one pocket, 17″ × 10″; cut along straight grain of fabric.

**3.** On the apron, stitch a narrow hem along the straight sides and the bottom.

**4.** Apply fold-over braid (use a zigzag stitch if your machine has one). First, outline pocket, enclosing raw edges with braid. Next, add braid to straight edge at top of apron.

**5.** Use remaining length of braid in a continuous strip. Measure off 30″ for one tie; at that mark, begin pinning braid to lower edge of apron curve. Work up to the neckline. Measure off 19″ for a neck strap; at that mark, continue pinning braid to other curve. When you finish, you will have 30″ of braid left for a second tie.

**6.** Begin stitching at one end of the braid; keep braid in folded position. Stitch along first tie, closing braid as you go. Continue along curve of apron, across neck strap, down opposite curve, and finally, along second tie. Make a knot in end of each tie to prevent fraying.

**7.** Position pocket on apron; have center of pocket running down center of apron. Stitch pocket at sides and across bottom. Stitch down center of pocket to divide it into two sections.

**10.** Follow Fig. 13 for assembling blocks for table runner. (Note: You may wish to arrange pieces for all three blocks before you begin to stitch.)

**11.** To assemble one block, first stitch small triangles (Fig. 10-d) to center square; press seams open.

**12.** Next, add middle-size triangles (Fig. 10-c); stitch and press seams open.

**13.** Stitch large triangles (Fig. 10-b) in place to finish the block; press seams open.

**14.** Topstitch along all seams; use a zigzag stitch if your machine has one.

**15.** Line up the three blocks and end pieces for the runner. Position blocks so that dominant color of center block is the same color as the end pieces. Join blocks and end pieces with ¼″ seams; press seams open.

**16.** Turn raw edges of runner ¼″ to wrong side. Stitch; use zigzag stitch if your machine has one (this reduces fraying of raw edge).

**17.** To make napkins, fold a narrow hem on all sides. Stitch and press.

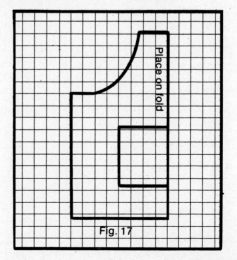

Fig. 17

Place on fold

## Yo-yo Pinafore

Pinafore is 19″ long from the shoulder; it's approximately a child's size 6. You can make it larger by adding more gathered circles—yo-yos—to the bottom and to the sides.

### Materials

- 2 yds. lightweight cotton, 45″ wide
- Thread
- 2 yds. ½″-wide grosgrain ribbon
- Cardboard for circle patterns

### Directions

**1.** From cardboard, cut two patterns for circles. Make one circle 5½″ in diameter, and make another 8″ in diameter.

**2.** Position circle patterns on fabric, trace around them, and cut. You need 60 small circles and 6 large ones.

**3.** Work with one circle at a time. Turn edge of fabric ¼″ to wrong side; press with fingers. Stitch along turned edge, using a long, loose stitch on the machine.

**4.** Pull ends of thread to gather fabric as tightly as possible, drawing outer edge of circle to center; raw edges will be inside the yo-yo. Tie thread ends to secure. (Note: Small finished yo-yo will be about 2½″ in diameter; large yo-yo will be about 4″.)

**5.** Repeat Steps 3 and 4 with all circles.

**6.** Arrange yo-yos according to Fig. 14, using large yo-yos at neckline. Front and back of pinafore are the same. Where edges touch, whip the yo-yos together with small hand stitches.

**7.** Join pinafore front to back at shoulders only.

**8.** Cut ribbon into four equal lengths. Attach one length to each of the four side edges for ties.

## Christmas Tree Apron

Apron is about 23″ long from shoulder; it's approximately a child's size 6.

### Materials

- ⅔ yd. striped denim, 36″ or 45″ wide
- 14″ by 12″ piece of red cotton for tree applique
- 14″ by 12″ piece of lightweight iron-on interfacing
- 6 yds. wide bias tape
- Thread
- Buttons, rickrack (small and medium widths), and embroidery floss for trim

### Directions

**1.** Enlarge pattern in Fig. 15, using a 1″ square for each square on the grid. Copy design to show applique and trim placement. Make a separate pattern for tree.

**2.** Use apron pattern to cut a front and a back from striped denim.

**3.** Join apron at shoulders.

**4.** Cover raw edges around apron and neckline with bias tape. Divide remaining tape into four equal lengths for apron ties. Fold tape and stitch

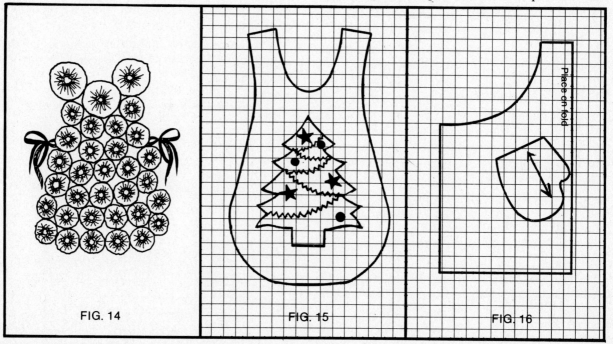

FIG. 14          FIG. 15          FIG. 16

along edges to close. Attach ties to the four sides of apron.

**5.** Use pattern to cut a Christmas tree from the iron-on interfacing. Then, iron tree to wrong side of red fabric. Cut around tree, allowing an extra ¼″ seam allowance.

**6.** Turn red fabric ¼″ to wrong side all around tree; clip seam allowance where necessary to let fabric lie flat.

**7.** Position tree on apron front and sew in place; topstitch by machine for a sturdy finish.

**8.** Trim tree, using buttons and rackrack. Outline buttons with chain stitches of embroidery floss.

## Boy's Apron

Apron is 20½″ long from top edge to bottom; neck straps tie in back so length can be adjusted.

### Materials

- ⅔ yd. fabric, 45″ wide
- 3½ yd. fold-over braid
- Thread

### Directions

**1.** Enlarge pattern in Fig. 16, using a 1″ square for each square shown on the grid. This gives you half the pattern. Draw pocket shape to mark placement on the pattern. Make a separate pattern for the pocket.

**2.** Fold fabric lengthwise, turning in one edge 15″ (fold will not be in center of fabric). Place long side of pattern along fold, with bottom edge of pattern near bottom edge of fabric. Pin and cut fabric. From remaining fabric, cut one pocket. (Note: Cut pocket so arrow is on straight grain of fabric—or, cut pocket so that any stripe or print matches stripe or print on the apron.)

**3.** Stitch a narrow hem along the straight sides and along the bottom.

**4.** Apply fold-over braid (use a zigzag stitch if your machine has one). First, outline the pocket, enclosing raw edges with braid. Next, add braid to straight edge at top of apron.

**5.** Divide remaining braid into two sections and cut.

**6.** Work with one section. Mark off 20″ for one back tie; at that mark, begin pinning braid to lower edge of apron curve. Work up to top edge; leave the remaining end for a neck tie.

**7.** Begin stitching at one end of the braid; keep braid in folded position as you work. Make a knot at each end of braid to prevent fraying.

**8.** Follow Steps 6 to 7 to apply second section of braid to opposite side of apron.

**9.** Position pocket on apron. Stitch around curves, leaving open the straight edge at top.

## Sports-Utility Vest

This is a loose-fitting vest; pattern is a medium size. You can alter size by adding to or subtracting from side seams; this may require a change in pockets also. Pockets can vary in size and number.

### Materials

- 2 yds. fabric, 45″ wide, for outside
- 2 yds. fabric, 45″ wide, for lining
- Thread
- 4 Gripper snaps
- 2 zippers, 7″ long, for pockets
- 2 swivel snaps (optional)

(Note: Vest is lined to the edge. You can use the same fabric for outside and lining, or you can use different fabrics.)

### Directions

**1.** Enlarge vest pattern in Fig. 18, using a 1″ square for each square on the grid. Mark top of vent on side seams (indicated by X on pattern). Mark position of snaps at front of vest (indicated by heavy dots on pattern). Mark position of finished pockets.

(Note: Narrow pocket Fig. 18-a and zippered pocket Figs. 18-b/c are used on both right and left sides of vest. The pockets Fig. 18-d are used on right side only; pocket Fig. 18-e is on left side only. Dotted lines on vest indicate stitching lines. Seam allowances are ⅝″ unless otherwise stated.)

**2.** From outside fabric, cut a complete vest and seven pockets. Cut two each of patterns Fig. 19-a, 19-b, 19-c and 19-d. Cut one of pattern Fig. 19-e.

**3.** From lining fabric, cut a complete vest.

**4.** Sew outside fabric together at shoulder seams; press seams open. Sew lining fabric together at shoulder seams; press seams open.

**5.** Place lining against the outside, right sides together. Pin along front, neck and armholes. Stitch up one front, around neck and down the other front. Stitch armhole edges together.

**6.** Turn vest to right side by pulling front sections through shoulder area. (Note: Side seams are not yet stitched.) Press.

**7.** Pin side seams together; join outside back to outside fronts and join lining back to lining fronts. Begin stitching on outside fabric at top of vent. Go up to the armhole and continue on around lining

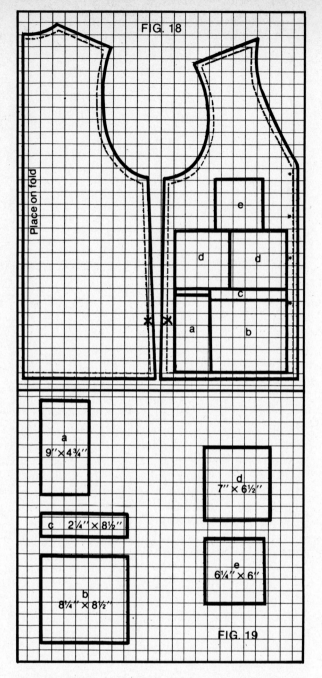

FIG. 18

Place on fold

e

d    d

c

a    b

a
9″ × 4¾″

c   2¼″ × 8½″

b
8¼″ × 8½″

d
7″ × 6½″

e
6¼″ × 6″

FIG. 19

side; press. Center folded edge along zipper, right side of fabric up; have ½″ of fabric extending beyond zipper at both ends. Stitch fabric to zipper. Next, work with bottom section (Fig. 19-b). Fold top edge to wrong side. Center fold along other side of zipper; stitch. Fold all outside edges of pocket ⅝″ to wrong side; press. Repeat Step 8 to make the second zippered pocket.

**10.** Work with remaining five pockets. With each, turn side and bottom edges to wrong side; press. Turn top edge 1″ to wrong side and press; then turn raw edge under ¼″ and stitch.

**11.** Position pockets according to diagram in Fig. 18. Topstitch all pockets in place. Stitch completely around zippered pockets; leave other pockets open at top.

**12.** Add four Gripper snaps to front of vest.

**13.** Add swivel snaps (optional). Sew one to side seam just above vent for holding gloves. Sew another inside a zippered pocket to hold a key ring.

## Petal Skirt for Tree

### Materials

- 1½ yds. velveteen or corduroy, 45″ wide, for top of petals
- 1½ yds. firm cotton, 45″ wide, for lining petals
- Thread
- 2 yds. grosgrain ribbon, ½″ wide, for ties

### Directions

**1.** Enlarge pattern in Fig. 21, using a 1″ square for each square shown on the grid. This gives you half a pattern.

**2.** To get a whole pattern, place the pattern half on a folded piece of paper (straight edge along fold); trace and cut. Open the pattern.

**3.** Use whole petal pattern, and cut 6 petals of top fabric and 6 petals of lining fabric. (Note: You can cut 3 petals across the 45″ width. Be sure to cut top fabric so the nap runs in the same direction on all petals.)

**4.** Handle each petal separately. Stitch top fabric to lining, right sides together; leave open the straight edge at top for turning.

**5.** Turn each petal to right side carefully to avoid wrinkling. Press. Close top edge with small hand stitches.

**6.** Cut ribbon into two lengths, 1 yd. each.

**7.** Work with one length of ribbon, and mark center with a pin. Then, measure 4½″ to each side of

in one stitching (outside of vest and lining are already joined at the armhole). Press seams open.

**8.** Turn raw edges of both outside and lining to wrong side along bottom edge and at vent (raw edges are sandwiched between layers of fabric). Edges of outside and lining should be even. Topstitch along all edges of vest; stitch around side vents as you go along bottom edges.

**9.** To make zippered pocket, first arrange the two zippers horizontally so that they open away from center. Keep zippers in this position as you make the two pockets; openings will be from center of vest when pockets are sewn in place. Take top section (Fig. 19-c). First, fold lower edge to wrong

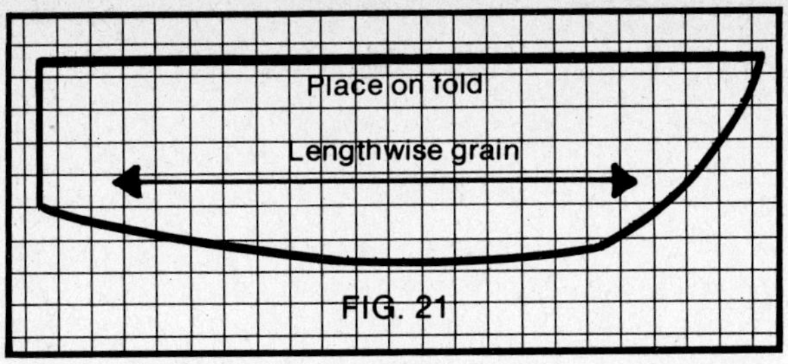

Place on fold
Lengthwise grain
FIG. 21

center and mark. This gives you three points where three petals will be attached.

**8.** Take one petal and mark center of top edge. Measure 3″ to each side of center and mark. Bring outside points to center, making a box pleat; pin. Place center of pleat at one of the three points on the ribbon. By hand, attach petal to ribbon, catching only the pleated section; leave rest of top edge free to form an overlap with adjoining petal.

**9.** Work with two more petals and attach them to the ribbon, following Step 8. When finished, you have a trio of petals attached to one length of ribbon; ends of ribbon will be used as ties.

**10.** Overlap top edges of petals and catch to the ribbon.

**11.** Work with remaining length of ribbon and petals. Follow Steps 7 through 10 to complete a second tie with a trio of petals.

**12.** To arrange skirt around tree, loosely tie one trio of petals along top of the tree holder (leave room for watering the tree). Add second trio of petals, so they fall between petals of first row.

## Seat Pad

**Materials**

- 1 foam pad, 15″ square, 2″ thick
- 1 yd. sturdy cotton fabric, 36″ or 45″ wide
- 1 zipper, 20″ long
- Thread

**Directions**

**1.** Follow dimensions and layout in Fig. 20 for cutting pieces from fabric. Use ½″ seam allowances unless otherwise stated.

**2.** Work with pocket piece. Turn top edge (16″ length) 1″ to wrong side; press. Turn raw edge under ¼″ and stitch.

**3.** Position wrong side of pocket against right side of front piece; have bottom and side edges even. Pin and stitch along bottom and side edges to hold pocket in place.

**4.** Make handles. Work with lengthwise edge, and turn fabric 1″ to wrong side; press. Turn in other edge 1″, overlapping first turn. Finally, turn raw edge under ¼″. Pin and stitch up center of handle along last fold.

**5.** Attach handles. Work with front section. Find center of top edge; mark. Measure 3″ to each side of center and mark. Attach one handle to the front piece; have ends of handle centered at the 3″ marks, right sides together. Pin and stitch across handle ends to hold them in place. Repeat this step, attaching second handle to back piece.

**6.** Sew zipper to top pieces. Along lengthwise edge of each top piece, turn fabric ½″ to wrong side. Position folded edge along center of zipper, leaving ½″ of fabric beyond zipper at each end. Pin and stitch. (Note: Folded edges meet at center to cover zipper.)

**7.** Make boxing. First, join bottom piece to side pieces; stitch with right sides together. Next, join top piece (with zipper) to side pieces.

**8.** Locate corner points on boxing; these are 15″ apart. Seams that join bottom and side pieces are two corner points. From each of these seams, measure up 15″ (into top piece) and mark; this gives you two more corner points. Press across boxing at corner points so that you join front and back pieces at the same location.

**9.** Join boxing to front section. Pin along edges, matching corners of front to corner folds on boxing. Stitch. Join boxing to back in the same way.

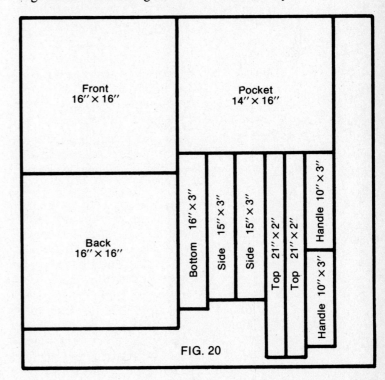

FIG. 20

# Denim Instructions

## How to prepare old denim

Wash jeans/overalls in hot water and detergent. If there are oil stains, put fabric in hot water and detergent and soak overnight; then, wash and use bleach according to directions. Dry fabric. Remove back pockets. Rip or cut leg sections into large strips. Stitch together enough long strips to get the length you need. Then, stitch these long strips together to get the width you need; arrange strips so crosswise seams are staggered and give an interesting patchwork effect. When you have joined enough strips, press the fabric, cut your pattern and sew. (Note: Overcast all raw edges to prevent fraying, especially if finished item will be washed.)

## Patched Shirt-Jacket

### Materials

- 1 printed cotton shirt
- Denim strips and patches to cover shirt
- Large spools of thread—one navy to match the denim, one in color to match background color of shirt
- Navy-colored shirt buttons (or use original shirt buttons)

### Directions

**1.** On shirt, open side seams and sleeve seams (to cuff). Where each sleeve joins cuff, clip seam of sleeve to stitching line. (This lets you turn seam edges to opposite side when you restitch them.)

**2.** If shirt has tails, turn tails to wrong side and press to make a straight line around bottom of shirt. Trim away excess fabric, leaving a ½" seam allowance.

**3.** Plan overall patchwork design. (We used narrow strips of dark denim at center front and wide strips of dark denim down center back and down center of sleeves.) The long triangular patches are cut from the crotch of jeans (left after you've taken the long strips). Work in small sections and keep denim smooth. Overlap patches and topstitch, using navy thread on the top of the machine and thread to match shirt on the bobbin; use a zigzag stitch if your machine has one. Along front edges and bottom of shirt, turn denim under so that it meets shirt fabric at the edge. Topstitch along edges. To cover top of each sleeve, first fit patches on the sleeve. At the armhole seam, stitch patches directly over the seam, carefully following the curved line. Trim away excess fabric. Next, fit patches to the shirt body and shoulder around the sleeve. Again, stitch directly over the armhole seam, following the curve. Trim fabric, leaving a raw edge of ½" beyond the stitching.

**4.** Close side seams and sleeve seams (to cuff) with straight stitches; follow the seam allowance originally used on the shirt. Overcast raw seam edges.

**5.** Cover cuffs and collar with denim; turn under raw edges and stitch. (If machine stitching makes fabric shift, you may want to use small hand stitches for this.)

**6.** Work buttonholes. Use original buttonholes as a guide and work new ones through all layers of fabric. (Jacket overlap will be reversed.)

**7.** Sew buttons in place.

## Denim Beret

### Materials

- Denim to cut two circles, 12½" in diameter. (You may want to use a foundation fabric and top it with denim patches.)
- Denim to make a bias strip, 1" wide, 23" long
- Length of ⅜"-wide elastic braid, about 24" long
- Thread

### Directions

**1.** Cut two circles from denim, 12½" in diameter. From the center of one, cut away a smaller circle, 6½" in diameter.

**2.** If you are using a foundation fabric, arrange denim patches on top and bottom sections of beret and stitch in place.

**3.** Cut and join bias to make a strip 1" wide and 23" long. Join ends of strip with ¼" seam to make a loop.

**4.** Pin bias loop to small circle opening of beret, right sides of fabric together. Stitch along edge with ¼" seam allowance. Press seam open. Turn bias at seam line so that it is flat against wrong side of beret. Press. Sew along raw edge of bias to form a tunnel (use zigzag stitch if your machine has one). Leave a small opening to insert elastic.

**5.** Stitch bottom of beret to top, right sides together and using a ¼″ seam allowance.

**6.** For medium head size (22″), cut a length of elastic 22″ long. (Cut a longer or shorter length as needed for other head sizes.) Work elastic through tunnel formed by bias strip. Overlap ends of elastic by 1″ and fasten temporarily with safety pin.

**7.** To adjust elastic for fit, try beret on head; shorten or lengthen elastic as needed. Then, stitch elastic at the overlap to hold it securely, and close opening along bias strip.

## Denim Doll

### Materials

- Denim to cut front and back of doll, each section 22″ long and 15″ wide, plus scraps of denim for center of eyes
- Pocket lining fabric from jeans for eyes and nose
- Denim or ⅜″ yd. printed cotton for overalls
- Small skein (2 or 2.5 oz.) 3-ply rug yarn for face embroidery and hair. (One skein makes long hair with braids for one doll or short hair for two dolls.)
- Large-eye needle for embroidering face
- Small piece of red cotton for heart applique (optional)
- Stuffing for doll. (It takes about 4 oz. of polyester fiberfill for one doll.)
- Navy thread for doll body; thread to match yarn hair

### Directions

**1.** Enlarge patterns in Fig. 1, using a 1″ square for each square shown on the grid. Use same doll pattern for front and back. Use full overall pattern for front; this includes the bib. Use only lower section of pattern (up to dotted line) for back; this omits the bib.

**2.** Cut doll. Use pattern to cut a front and a back; piece where necessary. (We cut front and back in three sections each—the head and two sides with a seam up center of body.) Allow ¼″ seam allowances wherever you piece sections.

**3.** Complete face. From pocket lining fabric, cut two circles (the size of a half-dollar) for eyes. Cut one circle (the size of a dime) for the nose. Position eye circles across center of face. Position center of nose 1″ below center of face. Stitch circles in place; use a zigzag stitch if your machine has one. Cut two eye "pupils" of dark denim; make these ½″ wide and 1¼″ long. Stitch in place on top of eye circles. Use rug yarn to embroider, by hand, the eyelashes and mouth. (If yarn is too thick to

pull through the denim, use only two strands.)

**4.** Piece body sections together so that you have a complete front and back. (If you have a seam up the front, leave it open part way for stuffing the doll; overcast open edges to prevent fraying.)

**5.** Stitch front and back together. If you do not have a center-front seam opening, leave an opening along one side for stuffing doll; overcast open edges to prevent fraying. Clip seam at inside curves (at neck, ankle, etc.). Press seam open. Turn doll to right side. With fingers, work seam to edge.

**6.** Stuff doll. Close opening with small hand stitches.

**7.** Make hair. First, open skein. (There are about 50 strands in the circle; length around circle is about 46″.)

*For long hair:* Cut away one strand of yarn (46″ long); divide this strand in two parts and put aside for tying braids. Stitch across the remaining 49 strands in the circle; keep them together so they measure about 3″ across. Stitch several times to secure. On one side of this stitching, measure down 1″ and cut across yarn. On other side, measure down 15″ from stitching and cut. This forms bangs and back hair. Find center of remaining length of yarn and stitch across. This forms hair for front and sides. Place first yarn piece so the 1″

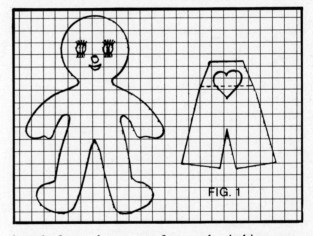

FIG. 1

length forms bangs on face and stitching runs along seam at top of head. Secure with hand stitches. Place second yarn piece on top of head so stitching forms a center part and just covers stitching along bangs. Secure with hand stitches. Arrange yarn to cover sides and back of head. Catch in place by hand. Divide strands and make braids at each side; tie each braid with a strand of yarn. Cut braid ends to make even.

*For short hair:* Divide circle of yarn into four equal sections, and mark with pins. Stitch across yarn at these marks, keeping strands together so they measure about 3″ across. Next, find the centers between adjacent lines of stitching; cut across yarn at these points. This gives you four identical sections, each about 11½″ long with a line of stitching at the center. Use two sections for one doll's hair. Handle the sections so that the stitching forms a center part. Place one section so stitching begins at seam on top of head and goes down back of head. Secure with hand stitches. Place second yarn section so stitching begins on face 1″ below seam at top of head and overlaps first yarn section. Secure with hand stitches. Arrange yarn at sides and back; secure with hand stitches.

**8.** Make overalls. Use pattern to cut a front (with bib) and a back. For straps, cut two strips of fabric, 1½″ wide and 8″ long. Make each strap by turning raw edges to wrong side along the 8″ length. Overlap raw edges and stitch up center of strap. Stitch front and back overall sections together, using ¼″ seam allowances. Hem around bib and pant legs by turning raw edges ¼″ to wrong side and stitching along the edges. Pin straps to bib at an angle; straps go over shoulders and meet in back where they are attached to overalls. Stitch straps at front. Mark position of straps at back; sew snaps for closure or secure with hand stitches. Note: For denim overalls, you may want to fringe some edges (bib, pant legs, straps) as we did. For this, machine stitch ¼″ from the cut edge and fringe. Also, cut straps only ¾″ wide.

## Open-top Tote

### Materials

- ⅞ yd. washable fabric for lining
- Denim patches to cover tote 18″ wide, 30″ long
- 2 strips of denim, 3″ wide, 15″ long for handles
- Thread in desired colors. On bobbin, use color that matches lining. On top of machine, use navy to match denim or use a color for contrast.

### Directions

**1.** Cut lining 18″ wide, 30″ long. Along each 18″-wide edge, make a ½″ turn to the wrong side; press. Measure down 13″ from each of these turns, and fold fabric, right sides together; press lightly. Measure in 1¾″ from each 30″-long side and fold fabric, right sides together; press lightly. These folds define the front, back, side panels and bottom of finished tote; use them as a guide to place denim patches in an interesting design.

**2.** Work with lining fabric right side down on flat surface. Arrange denim patches against wrong side of lining. (We used squares and rectangles for one tote, and curved patches with a red applique for the other. We also used the wrong side of some

denim patches to give more contrast.) Pin patches in place, trim away excess fabric. Along top edge of tote, turn patches under to line up with lining fabric; pin in place, but do not stitch until later. On rest of tote, stitch patches along the cut edges or stitch ¼″ from cut edges and fringe. (When tote is washed fringe will become fluffy.)

**3.** Make handles. On one strip, work with the 15″ length and turn one raw edge 1″ to wrong side; press. Turn other raw edge 1″, overlapping first turn; press. Turn the exposed raw edge under ⅜″; press. Stitch up center of handle along last turn; use zigzag or straight stitches. Make second handle in same manner.

**4.** Attach handles. Along top edge of tote (both front and back), mark center with a pin. Measure 2½″ to each side of center and mark with pins. Work with one handle. Center handle ends at the 2½″ marks along front edge; tuck handle ends between lining and outside, using ½″ seam allowances. Stitch all along front edge, catching handles in place; make extra stitches across handles to secure them. Stitch second handle to back edge in same manner.

**5.** Close side seams of tote with ¼″ seam allowances. Overcast raw edges.

**6.** Shape bag. With lining side out, flatten a triangle at the end of each side seam (seam will run up middle of triangle). Mark 1½″ along seam from tip of triangle; stitch a line across base of triangle at this mark (it will be 3″ across). Turn tote to right side. Use the last stitching as a guide and press 3″-wide side panels and a 3″-wide bottom on tote. Topstitch along these pressed edges.

## Collector's Tote

### Materials

- 1 jeans pant leg
- 1 strip of denim 3″ wide, 30″ long for strap
- Thread to match or contrast

### Directions

**1.** Cut off jeans pant leg 10″ from the bottom hem. Stitch cut edges together; overcast seam. (Hemmed edge of pant leg becomes top of tote.)

**2.** Shape bottom of bag. With tote wrong side out, flatten a triangle at each end of the bottom seam (seam will run through middle of triangle). Measure in about 1″ from each triangle tip and stitch across the triangles.

**3.** Make handle. Work with the 30″ length and turn one raw edge 1″ to wrong side; press. Turn other raw edge 1″, overlapping first turn; press.

Turn the exposed raw edge under ⅜″; press. Stitch along center of strap.

**4.** Position strap on bag, using ½″ seam allowances. Stitch across strap several times to secure.

## Tote with Pocket Flap

### Materials

- Denim for front panel, 14″ wide, 15″ long
- Denim for back panel and flap, 14″ wide, 27″ long
- Pocket for top of flap
- ¾ yd. firm fabric for lining
- 2 strips of denim, 3″ wide, 30″ long for the shoulder strap
- Thread to match or contrast

### Directions

**1.** Complete shoulder strap. Work along lengthwise edges. Turn raw edges of both strips ½″ to wrong side; press. Join strips by placing one on top of the other, wrong sides together; topstitch along edges.

**2.** Position strap at top edge of front panel. Keep strap ends ½″ away from each side; have raw edges of strap even with raw edge of panel. (Note: Keep same side of strap up at both ends.) Stitch strap in place, ½″ from raw edge. Turn handle up. Make a fold across front panel, turning top edge 1″ to wrong side. Stitch along folded edge, catching handle as you go.

**3.** Shape tote at bottom of both front and back panels. Along each bottom edge, measure in 4½″ from both sides; along both sides, measure up 3″ from bottom edge. (See Fig. 2.) Mark points, draw lines connecting the points and cut away the resulting triangles. Along cut edges, measure up 1″ from bottom edge; then, mark off an additional ½″ for a dart. Measure another 1″ and then another ½″ for a second dart. Draw in darts, 2½″ deep from cut edge. Stitch darts. Press darts on front panel toward center of panel, and press darts on back panel toward the sides; this helps reduce seam bulk when panels are stitched together.

**4.** Join front and back panels. Pin right sides together. Begin stitching 1½″ below top edge of front panel. (This opening at top edge is left until lining is added.) Stitch down one side, across bottom and up other side, ending 1½″ below top edge of front panel.

**5.** Position pocket on top of flap. Topstitch in place.

**6.** Make lining. Cut front panel 14″ wide and 14½″ long. Cut back panel 14″ wide, 27″ long.

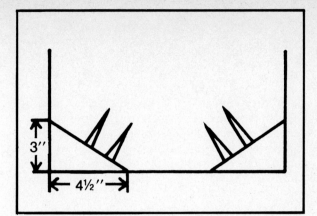

FIG. 2

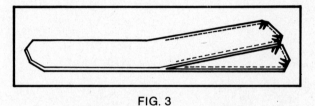

FIG. 3

Shape bottom of lining panels, following directions in Step 3. Join front and back panel along sides; leave bottom seam open for turning tote to right side.

**7.** Shape flap (on both tote and lining) by cutting off a triangle at each corner. Do this by measuring in 4½″ from each side, and down each side 3″ from top edge. Mark, draw connecting lines, and cut away resulting triangles.

**8.** Join lining to tote. Work with tote and lining both wrong side out. First, line up top edges of front panels, right sides together; have raw seam edges together. Stitch, using a ½″ seam allowance. Press seam allowance down, toward bottom of bag. Next, position lining on top of tote; have flaps extended, right sides of flaps together. (See Fig. 3.) Pin along edges of flaps, keeping strap away from seam line. Begin stitching lining to tote at one side. Overlap stitching already completed; this will catch all layers of fabric just below edge of front panels. Stitch up one side, across top of flap and down other side, overlapping stitching. Press seam open. Turn tote to right side through opening in lining. Press. Topstitch along edge of flap. Close lining seam with small hand stitches.

# Quilling Instructions

After practicing the basic rolling technique and the 14 basic shapes, you're ready to begin the quilling projects. The instructions for the projects have been organized in order of difficulty, so you might want to start at the beginning and work your way through to the end. Each set of instruc- tions lists the shapes you'll need to make, how many of each shape, and the length of the strip of paper needed to make the shape the right size. You'll find step-by-step instructions for assembling the basic shapes to form the design. Patterns for each project show how to assemble the pieces.

**Fantasy Flowers**

**Mini-flakes**

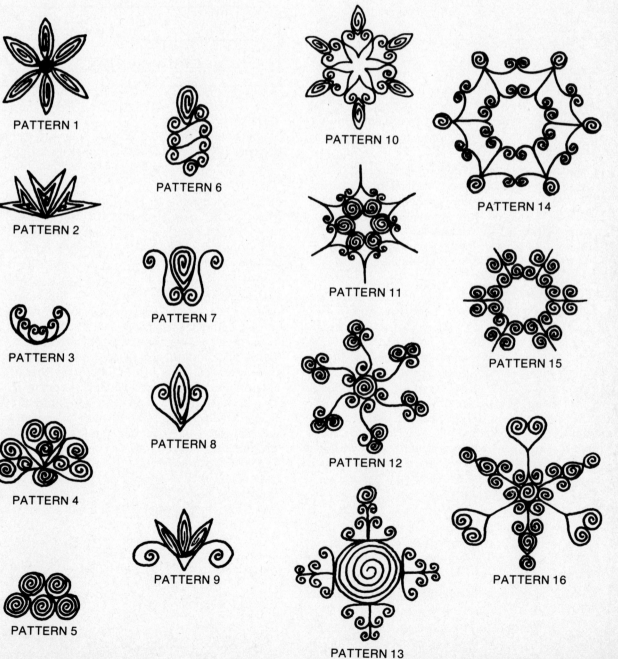

PATTERN 1

PATTERN 6

PATTERN 2

PATTERN 7

PATTERN 3

PATTERN 8

PATTERN 4

PATTERN 9

PATTERN 5

PATTERN 10

PATTERN 11

PATTERN 12

PATTERN 13

PATTERN 14

PATTERN 15

PATTERN 16

## Fantasy Flowers

There are limitless variations of fantasy flowers, but try these first, then use your own imagination to come up with other designs. (Described here are nine different flowers used for plaque and frame. The sizes and number of petals can be varied, but follow the pattern for exact duplication.)

### Materials

- Assorted colored papers
- Glue

### Directions

Following instructions for 14 basic shapes, make shapes as follows:

**1.** Following Pattern 1, arrange six 4″ eyes around one 3″ peg; glue tips of eyes onto peg.

**2.** Following Pattern 2, position three 5″ pinched hearts, points together; glue only where tips meet.

**3.** Following Pattern 3, nest three 3″ scrolls, backs together, and glue.

**4.** Following Pattern 4, glue three 2″ circles inside three 4″ hearts. Place points of hearts together and glue where tips and sides touch. Position and glue hearts on a 3″ circle of contrasting color.

**5.** Following Pattern 5, form semicircle around one 4″ peg with four 4″ pegs; glue.

**6.** Following Pattern 6, stack three 2½″ S's horizontally and glue where curled ends touch. Place 3″ tear and 2″ circle above S's and a 2″ circle below S's; glue where ends touch.

**7.** Following Pattern 7, glue one end of two 2½″ S's back-to-back; allow other ends to curl out open. Place one 3½″ tear, point down, within glued end of S's; glue at contact point.

**8.** Following Pattern 8, place one 4″ thin eye inside 3″ heart; glue at contact point and where curled ends of heart meet sides of eye.

**9.** Following Pattern 9, glue three 4″ thin eyes together and place within a 4″ wide V; glue.

## Plaque

### Materials

- Oval plaque (6″ × 4″) with beveled edge
- Gold and white paint
- Fantasy flowers (an assortment)
- Long green and brown quilling strips
- White glue

### Directions

**1.** Paint beveled edge of plaque gold; antique flat surface white.

**2.** Glue several fantasy flowers onto flat surface in a pleasing arrangement.

**3.** Connect flowers with swirly stems and fill in open spaces with many long, delicately curved tendrils.

## Frame

Follow directions for plaque, except use a frame and decorate it.

## Mini-flakes

Try quilling these mini-flakes and hang as Christmas ornaments from the fireplace or in windows throughout the house. Or, use in mobile with large snowflakes.

### Materials

- White or ecru paper
- White glue

### Directions

Following instructions for 14 basic shapes, make shapes as follows:

**1.** According to Pattern 10, make twelve 2½″ glued V shapes; nest two together to make six sets. Arrange in a circle, curled ends touching. Glue.

**2.** According to Pattern 11, arrange six 2½″ hearts in a circle, points inward. Glue a 3″ eye into curled ends of each heart. Glue hearts together where sides touch.

**3.** According to Pattern 12, position and glue six 3″ circles in a ring. Glue six 2½″ open V shapes, points outward, evenly around ring of circles.

**4.** According to Pattern 13, arrange six 2½″ S shapes around a 3″ circle; glue. Glue two 2½″ circles to the top end of each S shape.

**5.** According to Pattern 14, roll one 5″ loose circle. Place four 2″ scrolls, lying on their backs, evenly around circle; glue center back of scroll to circle. Place two 2″ nested glued V shapes, stems inward, inside each scroll and glue. (One nested V point may be topped by a 2″ circle to facilitate hanging.)

**6.** According to Pattern 15, place six 2½″ glued V shapes in a circle, stems outward; glue where curled ends touch. Glue a 2″ open V on top of each stem, and glue curled ends of open V's where they touch. Top each point of open V with a 2″ circle.

**7.** According to Pattern 16, make a 3″ circle; place

eight 2½″ glued V shapes around it, alternating stem up, stem down. Place and glue a 2½″ heart, point down, on each of the glued V stems. Glue a 2½″ tear, point up, on each of the glued V curled ends. Top tear shape with a 2″ circle.

## Mobile

### Materials

- Cardboard strip
- Stapler (optional)
- Gold spray paint
- 5 Snowflake designs
- Fine gold thread
- Tape
- Gold braid
- 7 Mini-flake designs
- Trim
- White glue

### Directions

1. Fashion a ring about 8″ in diameter and about 1″ wide from cardboard—you'll need a piece 25″ long. Or piece and staple from pieces of cardboard.

2. Make a second ring 4″ in diameter and 2″ wide from a piece of cardboard—you'll need a piece 12½″ long.

3. Spray both rings with gold paint, inside and out.

4. Make five Snowflake patterns and attach fine gold thread to one point for hanging. Hang at regular intervals (every 5″) around larger ring on 2″- to 4″-long threads. Attach threads to inside of ring with tape.

5. Use flat ½″ gold braid, cut into four strips about 4″ long to connect smaller ring to larger one. (Both rings should be at the same level, at the top, so be sure the braid is taut enough.) Attach another strip to span the inner ring. The mini-flakes hanging in the center ring will be hung from this. Use thin gold thread fastened to the inside of the outer ring to hang the mobile.

6. Make three mini-flakes to hang on very short threads from inner circle (¼″ to ¾″); make three more to hang at a level about equal to the lower edge of the large flakes. Make one more to hang from a thread suspended from the braid spanning the inner circle.

7. Cover rings, inside and out, with metallic trim, lace, braid, ribbon or any combination of trims. Choose trim which is the same width or slightly wider than the rings. Attach it with white glue. Allow to dry thoroughly.

## Snowflake #1

Make Snowflakes to hang as individual tree ornaments, or follow directions for combining with mini-flakes to form mobile.

### Materials

- White or ecru paper
- White glue

Following instructions for 14 basic shapes, make shapes as follows:

| number | strip length | shape |
|--------|--------------|-------|
| 6 | 2″ | S's |
| 18 | 3″ | eyes |
| 6 | 3″ | circles |
| 12 | 2½″ | S's |
| 6 | 1½″ | glued V's |
| 6 | 2″ | circles |
| 6 | 5″ | circles |

### Directions

1. Following Pattern 17, arrange and glue six 2″ S shapes in circular design.

2. Form a "Y-shape" with three eyes according to Fig. 3; glue together where tips touch. Make six groups.

3. Place the Y-shapes made in Step 2 around the center S's, bridging the outside ends of the S's; glue.

4. Position 3″ circles where two Y-shapes join over the center S's.

5. Arrange and glue 2½″ S's to connect tips of the Y-shape and circles. Insert glued V shapes between two S's that connect circle to Y-shape. Top glued V with 2″ circle.

6. Glue 5″ circle to junction of two S's and Y-shape.

PATTERN 17

160

## Snowflake #2

**Materials**

- White or ecru paper
- White glue

Following instructions for 14 basic shapes, make shapes as follows:

| number | strip length | shape |
|---|---|---|
| 6 | 2″ | S's |
| 24 | 3″ | eyes |
| 6 | 3″ | circles |
| 12 | 2½″ | S's |
| 12 | 1½″ | glued V's |
| 6 | 2″ | circles |

**Directions**

**1.** Follow steps 1 through 4 for Snowflake #1; eliminate steps 5 and 6.

**2.** Following Pattern 18, invert 2½″ S's so that curled ends are downward over tip of Y-shape.

**3.** Insert glued V shapes on 3″ circles and between two S shapes. Top with 2″ circle.

**4.** Position and glue V shapes on top of S shapes. Top with 3″ eyes.

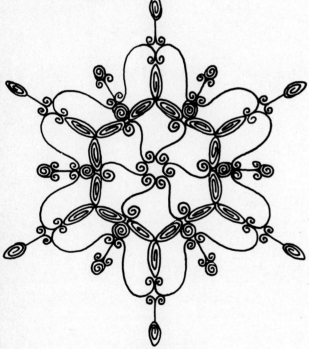

PATTERN 18

## Snowflake #3

**Materials**

- White or ecru paper
- White glue

Following instructions for 14 basic shapes, make shapes as follows:

| number | strip length | shape |
|---|---|---|
| 6 | 2½″ | hearts |

| 1 | 3½″ | circle |
| 6 | 3″ | circles |
| 6 | 2″ | glued V's |
| 6 | 3″ | eyes |
| 12 | 2½″ | S's |
| 6 | 2½″ | circles |

**Directions**

**1.** Arrange hearts, point side inward, evenly around 3½″ circle; glue.

**2.** Insert 3″ circle into curled ends of hearts; glue.

**3.** Top stem of glued V shape with 3″ eye; glue.

**4.** Following Pattern 19, place glued V with eye between 3″ circles. Glue where ends touch.

**5.** Connect top of eye and 3″ circle with S shape.

**6.** Place 2½″ circle at each high point where S shapes meet; glue.

PATTERN 19

## Snowflake #4

**Materials**

- White or ecru paper
- White glue

Following instructions for 14 basic shapes, make shapes as follows:

| number | strip length | shape |
|---|---|---|
| 6 | 2½″ | hearts |
| 1 | 3½″ | circle |
| 6 | 3″ | eyes |
| 6 | 2″ | glued V's |
| 12 | 3″ | circles |
| 12 | 2″ | S's |
| 6 | 3″ | diamonds |

161

## Directions

**1.** Arrange hearts, point side inward, evenly around 3½″ circle; glue.

**2.** Insert eyes between curled ends of hearts and glue.

**3.** Following Pattern 20, connect and glue tops of hearts together with glued V shapes.

**4.** Top each eye and glued V with a 3″ circle.

**5.** Following pattern, position and glue S shapes on top of each 3″ circle; glue tops of S shapes together.

**6.** Insert and glue diamonds between curled ends of glued S's.

PATTERN 20

### Snowflake #5

**Materials**

- White or ecru paper
- White glue

Following instructions for 14 basic shapes, make shapes as follows:

| number | strip length | shape |
|---|---|---|
| 13 | 3″ | circles |
| 6 | 2½″ | glued V's |
| 6 | 2″ | open V's |
| 12 | 3″ | eyes |
| 12 | 2″ | S's |
| 6 | 2″ | scrolls |
| 6 | 2½″ | circles |

**Directions**

**1.** Arrange and glue six 3″ circles around a seventh 3″ circle to form center.

**2.** Position glued V's around center, curled ends touching circles; glue.

**3.** Following Pattern 21, balance and glue an open V atop each glued V. (Arrange them so that the ends of the open V's don't quite touch.) Place 3″ circles to connect the ends of open V shapes; glue.

**4.** Top circles and stems of open V shapes with eyes; glue.

**5.** Connect circles and eyes (atop the open V's) with S shapes, according to pattern. Glue S shapes together at tops.

**6.** Top glued S's with scrolls lying on their backs; glue into position.

**7.** Cradle a 2½″ circle in each scroll; glue.

PATTERN 21

### Snowflake #6

**Materials**

- White or ecru paper
- White glue

Following instructions for 14 basic shapes, make shapes as follows:

| number | strip length | shape |
|---|---|---|
| 18 | 1½″ | glued V's |
| 18 | 3″ | eyes |
| 12 | 2″ | scrolls |
| 6 | 4″ | circles |
| 6 | 2½″ | glued V's |
| 6 | 2″ | glued V's |
| 6 | 2″ | circles |

**Directions**

**1.** Arrange six 1½″ glued V's, curled ends inward, evenly in a circle; glue where ends touch.

**2.** Arrange three 3″ eyes in Y-shape (see Fig. 3 for Snowflake #1); make six groups.

**3.** Following Pattern 22, bridge glued V shapes with Y-shapes.

**4.** Place and glue 1½″ glued V's onto eyes above stem of center glued V's.

**5.** Connect tip of Y-shapes and ends of outermost glued V shapes with scrolls.

**6.** Top curled scroll ends over glued V's with circles; glue.

**7.** Nest glued V shapes: Insert and glue stem of 2½″ glued V into curled end of 2″ glued V; fit 2″ glued V into curled end of 1½″ glued V. Make six groups.

**8.** Top curled ends of scrolls over Y-shape with assembly of nested glued V's, curled ends inward. Top with a 2″ circle; glue.

| number | strip length | shape | color |
|---|---|---|---|
| 8 | 2½″ | S's | green |
| 6 | 2½″ | scrolls | green |
| 8 | 3″ | circles | green |
| 1 | 2½″ | open V | green |
| 6 | 3½″ | diamonds | green |
| 2 | 4″ | circles | green |
| 1 | 5″ | diamonds | green |
| 5 | 3″ | eyes | green |

PATTERN 23

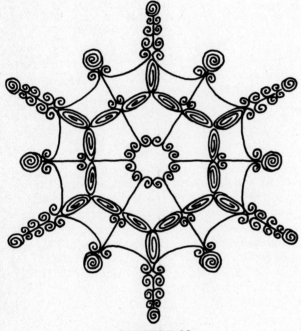

PATTERN 22

## Christmas Tree

### Materials

- Colored papers
- Glue
- Gold cord
- Sequins or glass beads (optional)
- Cardboard (optional)
- Gold spray paint (optional)
- Gold cord (optional)

Following instructions for 14 basic shapes, make shapes as follows:

| number | strip length | shape | color |
|---|---|---|---|
| 2 | 2½″ | ½ feathers | brown |
| 1 | 4″ | eye | brown |
| 2 | 3″ | scrolls | brown |

### Directions

**1.** Following Pattern 23, make trunk first. Glue two ½ feathers atop 4″ eye. Glue 3″ scrolls back to back and attach to ½ feather.

**2.** Build outline of tree from bottom up: Use two S's, six scrolls, eight 3″ circles and one open V. Glue together.

**3.** Fill in design with remainder of pieces. (Note: You can create your own center design if you wish.)

**4.** Working from bottom of design up: three 3½″ diamonds, two 4″ circles, two S's, two 3½″ diamonds, two S's, one 5″ diamond, two S's, two 3″ eyes, one 3½″ diamond and three 3″ eyes. (Note: You can decorate with gold cord, sequins or glass beads, etc., if desired.)

**5.** Entire tree can be placed in a strip of cardboard formed into an oval. Spray cardboard gold and finish the raw edges with gold cord. Fit the tree inside and glue generously. Allow to dry thoroughly. Attach gold cord to top of oval to hang.

# Lighted Hoop Instructions

## Lighted Christmas Hoop

**Materials**

- string of miniature lights
- rug yarns
- blunt-end tapestry needle
- scissors
- a pair of metal hoops—8″, 10″ or 12″ in diameter. These can be purchased in craft shops. Or you can make them of number 9- to 12-gauge steel wire, soldered to form hoops. Or the same gauge aluminum wire, ends held together with masking tape. Either wire is available at hardware stores.

**Directions**

*To cover string of lights with a 4-strand braid:*

1. Cut two lengths of yarn at least 4′ long.

2. Place the center of each yarn across the light cord—at the base of the last light on the string (Fig. 1). Position yarns so they crisscross over the light cord.

3. Holding these yarns in place with the left hand, use the right hand to pick up the top yarn on the left side (b in Fig. 1), bring it under and over the light cord. Then bring back under light cord, up between the two yarns on the right side and back over the cord returning to the left side (Fig. 2).

4. Holding these yarns in place with the right hand, use the left hand to move the top yarn at your right (as in Fig. 2) under the cord, up between the two yarns, over the cord returning it to the right side (Fig. 3). This 4-strand braiding sounds more complicated than it really is. Once you get yarns in hand, you'll find that the braiding is easy. Especially when you establish the routine:
   - take the top of the 4 yarns (the higher one)
   - go under the light cord
   - come up between the two yarns on opposite side
   - over the light cord to starting side of yarn.
Continue on, alternating sides each time (Fig. 4).

5. When the yarns become too short to work with, add on the new yarns the same way you began—by placing new yarns over the light cord and braiding over the loose ends to hide them. Trimming the ends to tapered points and different lengths reduces the bulk (Fig. 5).

6. Occasionally it will be desirable to double the light cord—leaving a light on the end of it (Fig. 6). We show two ways to do this. If you want the lights to alternate, you need to take an extra tuck (b). Begin the new yarns at the bottom light (a) and work the braid up the cord to the point where the braiding ended previously. Loose yarn ends may be concealed by braiding over them or by using a tapestry needle to weave them back into the braid.

7. To end the braiding at the plug, wrap one yarn around the braid several times, then use tapestry needle to weave it back into the braid. The remaining three yarns may then be trimmed closely.

*To cover the metal hoops:*

Measure off two yarns that are four times the length of the circumference of each hoop. Begin at any point on the hoop, placing the center of the yarns over it as in Step 1 and continue with the same steps as you used for covering the cord. When the hoop is covered, leave the yarn ends. You'll need them for assembling.

*To assemble hoops and cord:*

Thread one of the yarn ends through a tapestry needle and sew the hoops together at that point. At the point where the hoops meet, drape the covered cord into a pleasing arrangement. The cord may be arranged in loops of varying sizes—some can be bunched together at the top, some larger loops hang freely, some lights hang straight down (see photo). When you have the arrangement you like, attach by using the yarn ends and tapestry needle. Take care not to pierce the cord itself with the needle.

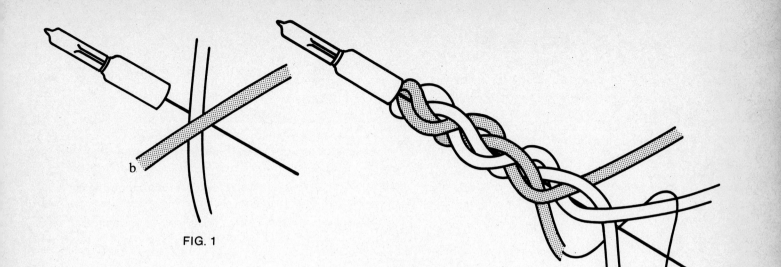

FIG. 1

FIG. 4

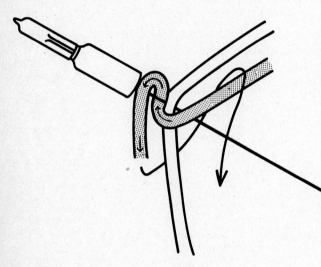

FIG. 2

FIG. 5

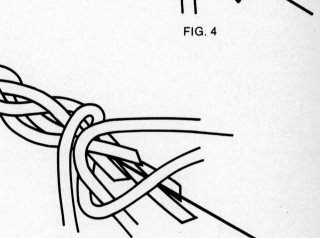

FIG. 3

FIG. 6

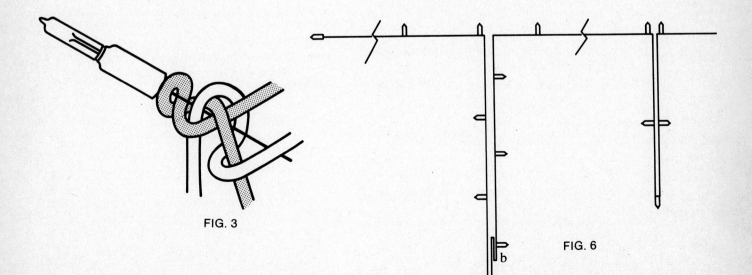

# Tree Trim Instructions

These patterns are half size. To enlarge any of the ornaments (angels look well in assorted sizes), draw 1- to 1½-inch squares on paper and copy pattern lines as they appear in our smaller blocks.

## Pixie or Elf

### Materials

- red or green felt and thread
- pink felt and thread for sewing face
- red, black embroidery floss
- stuffing
- fake fur for elf beard
- white pompon tassel
- gold thread for hanging

### Directions

**1.** Pin body pattern to two thicknesses of red or green felt. Machine stitch close to edge of pattern, using it as a guide.

**2.** Stitch from "ear to ear" around body; leave top of head open. Trim away excess fabric to within ⅛" of seam. (Cap will be stitched and trimmed later.)

**3.** Cut face from pink felt; hand stitch to body and embroider facial features.

**4.** Stuff, using less stuffing in head so it will be easier to complete stitching.

**5.** With pattern pinned in place, machine stitch around head and cap. Trim to ⅛" from stitching line.

**6.** Hand stitch beard in place for elf.

**7.** Sew tassel onto end of cap, then fold cap down and tuck into position.

**8.** Stitch gold thread loop to top of head to hang.

## Wise Men.

### Materials

- gold, turquoise, purple and pink felt and thread
- chalk
- blue, black, red, green, yellow, gold, purple embroidery floss
- brass beads, gold stars
- stuffing
- white felt and thread
- gold thread for hanging

### Directions

**1.** Lay body pattern on a 7×4" rectangle of felt, single thickness. Trace around it with chalk.

**2.** Cut out the face pieces, gifts, and hands; position and sew them on within the chalk outline.

**3.** Embroider facial features, hat trim and sew on the "jewels." Keep within chalk outline.

**4.** Place this single thickness, completed except for beard, on a second 7×4" rectangle of matching felt.

**5.** Using the chalk outline, or the pattern pinned in place, as a guide, sew around figure, leaving 1½" opening below the left arm.

**6.** Trim to ⅛" from stitching line, leaving a little excess near the opening to be trimmed later.

**7.** Stuff, stitch opening closed and trim.

**8.** Hand stitch beard into place.

**9.** Attach gold thread loop to center back of head for hanging.

## Angel

### Materials

- scraps of print fabric
- pink felt and pink thread for sewing face
- red, blue, pink, brown embroidery floss
- approximately 6" pre-gathered lace
- stuffing (polyester filling from department store works well)
- white felt and thread
- silver thread for hanging

### Directions

**1.** Using body pattern, cut a front and a back body piece from print fabric. Add extra fabric (3/16" or so) for seams.

**2.** Cut face from pink felt. Hand stitch face to front of body pieces using small running stitch. Embroider facial features.

**3.** Machine stitch lace to front body piece (around the head), right sides together, placing straight edge of lace along the ¼" seamline.

**4.** Pin back of doll to front, right sides together. Stitch all around doll except for 1½" below left arm. Clip inside curves (such as neck, underarm) so they will lie flat when turned.

**5.** Turn and stuff. Close seam securely with small slip-stitch.

**6.** Pin wing pattern to two thicknesses of white felt. Machine stitch close to edge of pattern, using it as a guide.

**7.** Cut out wings; trim to ⅛″ from stitching line.

**8.** Hand stitch wings to back of angel.

**9.** Sew a silver thread loop at center back of head so that angel tilts just a bit when hanging.

## Santa

### Materials

- red and pink felt and thread
- blue, black, red embroidery floss
- stuffing
- white felt and thread
- white glue
- brass beads for buttons
- gold thread for hanging

### Directions

**1.** Follow steps 1 through 5 as for pixie.

**2.** Cut out and glue on white felt beard, suit and cap trimmings.

**3.** Sew "buttons" on, knotting the thread up under the beard.

**4.** Attach gold thread for hanging.

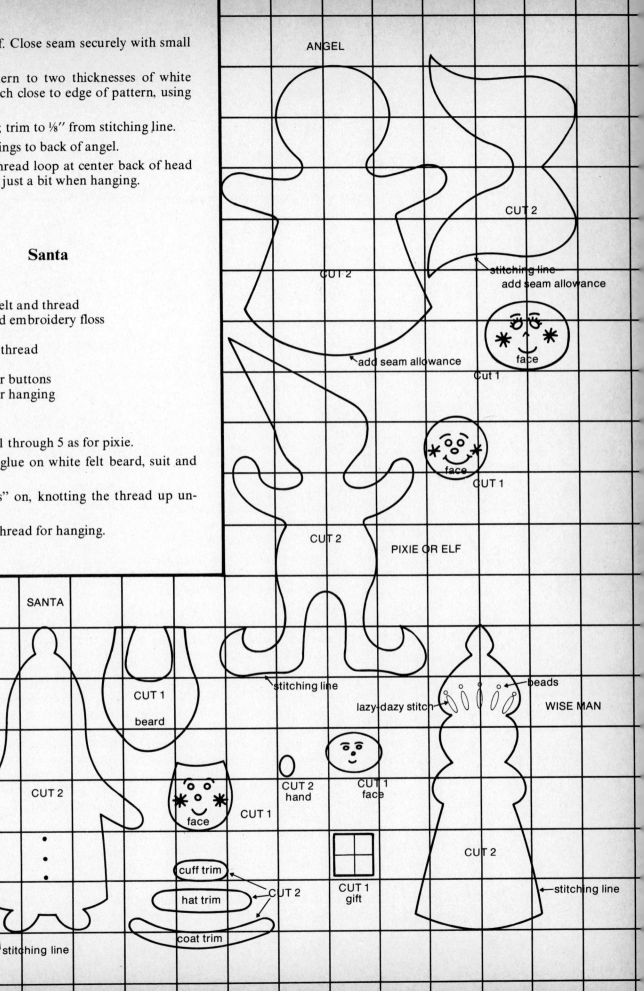

# Knitting Instructions

## General Information

### Knitting Abbreviations

dec—decrease; dp—double-pointed; K—knit; P—purl; st(s)—stitch(es); inc—increase; sl—slip; tog—together

### To block finished items

Press on wrong side with a steam iron, being careful not to stretch patterns out of shape.

### To wash items

Wash in cool water, using special wool detergent. Squeeze dry and blot between towels. Lay out on a flat surface to dry. When dry, press on the wrong side with a steam iron, being careful not to stretch patterns out of shape. *Do not dry clean,* as this will remove the lanolin in the yarn. (Note: If you cannot find yarn suitable for fisherman-type designs locally, send a stamped, self-addressed envelope for prices to: Janknits, Ingomar, Montana 59039.)

## Man's Pullover

### Sizes

Directions are for small size (42). Changes for medium (44) and large (46) are in parentheses.

| Measurements (when blocked) | Sm. | Med. | Lg. |
|---|---|---|---|
| Chest | 42″ | 44″ | 46″ |
| Length to underarm | 17″ | 18″ | 19″ |
| Sleeve length, neck to wrist | 29″ | 29″ | 30″ |
| Sweater length, shoulder to bottom | 29″ | 30″ | 31″ |

### Materials

10 (10-11) 4-oz. skeins Janknits oiled yarn or 20 (20-22) 2-oz. skeins Bernat Blarney-Spun yarn; straight knitting needles No. 6 and 10; any double-pointed needle smaller than a size 10 to use as a stitch holder in making the patterns; set of double-pointed needles size 6 for neck ribbing.

### Gauge

With No. 10 needles and using the stockinette stitch (K 1 row, P 1 row), 7 sts = 2″; 5 rows = 1″.

### Helpful hints

*To increase:* Increase stitches on last row of ribbing by first knitting in the back loop of a knit stitch; then with the stitch still on the needle, knit in the front loop of the same stitch. When increasing above the ribbing on the sleeve, increase on the right side by knitting in the back loop of the first stitch on the needle; then with the stitch still on the needle, knit in the front loop of the same stitch. On the other side of the sleeve, increase in the same manner on the last stitch on the needle.

*To join new ball of yarn:* Join yarn at edge of the piece so that yarn ends can be pulled into the seams.

*To sew pieces together:* When you finish a piece, leave about a 20″ tail of yarn for sewing together. Using a blunt needle (tapestry needle) and working from the right side, bring needle up through first stitch on the left edge. Insert the needle down through center of first stitch on right edge, pass under 2 rows, pull yarn through to right side. Insert needle in center of stitch on corresponding row of left side (same place you came out on previous stitch on that side), pass under 2 rows, drawing yarn through to right side. Continue working from side to side, being careful not to pull the stitches too tight.

*To pick up neck stitches:* Use a crochet hook. Slip hook into stitches along edge, catch yarn and pull through. Transfer stitches to needle by sliding them off the end of the crochet hook onto the needle.

## Patterns

**Pattern 1:** Twisted ribbing

**Row 1:** *K 1 in back loop of stitch, P 1*. Repeat from * to * across.
**Row 2:** Repeat row 1, knitting in the back loop of the K sts and purling the P sts.
Repeat these rows for pattern 1.

**Pattern 2:** Bramble stitch

**Row 1:** (right side) Purl across.
**Row 2:** *K 1, P 1, K 1 in first st, P 3 tog*. Repeat from * to * across. (There will be 2 more sts on this row than on row 1.)
**Row 3:** Purl across.
**Row 4:** *P 3 tog, K 1, P 1, K 1 in next st*. Repeat from * to * across.
Repeat these rows for pattern 2.

**Pattern 3:** Herringbone variation

**Row 1:** P 2, sl next 2 sts onto a dp needle and hold in back of work, K next st, then K the 2 sts from the dp needle, sl next st onto a dp needle and hold in front of work, K next 2 sts, then K st from dp needle, P 2.
**Row 2:** K 2, P 6, K 2.
**Row 3:** P 2, K 6, P 2,
**Row 4:** K 2, P 6, K 2.
**Row 5:** P 2, sl next st onto a dp needle and hold in front of work. K next 2 sts, then K the st from dp needle, sl next 2 sts onto a dp needle and hold in back of work, K next st, then K the 2 sts from the dp needle, P 2.
**Row 6:** Repeat row 2.
**Row 7:** Repeat row 3.
**Row 8:** Repeat row 2.
Repeat these rows for pattern 3.

**Pattern 4:** Cable variation

**Row 1:** P 1 (2-3), K 1, P 2, K 1, P 1 (2-3).
**Row 2:** K 1 (2-3), P 1, K 2, P 1, K 1 (2-3).
**Row 3:** Repeat row 1.
**Row 4:** Repeat row 2.
**Row 5:** (twist) P 1 (2-3), sl next st onto dp needle and hold in front of

work, K third st on left hand needle and leave on needle, P first two sts on left hand needle and slide off needle as they are worked, slide third st off needle, K st from dp needle, P 1 (2-3).

**Row 6:** Repeat row 2.
**Row 7:** Repeat row 1.
**Row 8:** Repeat row 2.
Repeat these rows for pattern 4.

(Note: It will be handy to remember that this cable is twisted on the same row that the circle is completed in pattern 3. Also, the number of stitches on either side of the cable will vary depending on which size you are knitting.)

**Pattern 5:** Woven cable

**Row 1:** P 1, K 18, P 1.
**Row 2:** K 1, P 18, K 1.
**Row 3:** (first twist) P 1, *sl next 3 sts onto dp needle and hold in back of work, K next 3 sts, K the 3 sts from the dp needle*. Repeat from * to * twice more, P 1.
**Row 4:** Repeat row 2.
**Row 5:** Repeat row 1.
**Row 6:** Repeat row 2.
**Row 7:** (second twist) P 1, K 3, *sl next 3 sts onto a dp needle and hold in front of work, K next 3 sts, K the 3 sts from dp needle*. Repeat from * to * once more, K 3, P 1.
**Row 8:** Repeat row 2.
Repeat these rows for pattern 5.

## Directions

**Back:** With No. 6 needles, cast on 86 (90-94) sts. Work in twisted ribbing (pattern 1) for 2″. On last row of ribbing inc 8 sts evenly spaced across row. 94 (98-102) sts on needle. Change to No. 10 needles and begin pattern.

**Row 1:** (right side) K 1, work first row of pattern 2 across next 17 sts, K 1, work first row of pattern 3 across next 10 sts, K 1 in back loop, work first row of pattern 4 across next 6 (8-10) sts, K 1 in back loop, work first row of pattern 5 across next 20 sts, K 1 in back loop, work first row of pattern 4 across next 6 (8-10) sts, K 1 in back loop, work first row of pattern 3 across next 10 sts, K 1, work first row of pattern 2 across next 17 sts, K 1.
**Row 2:** P 1, work second row of pat-tern 2 across next 17 sts, P 1, work second row of pattern 3 across next 10 sts, P 1 in back loop, work second row of pattern 4 across next 6 (8-10) sts, P 1 in back loop, work second row of pattern 5 across next 20 sts, P 1 in back loop, work second row of pattern 4 across next 6 (8-10) sts, P 1 in back loop, work second row of pattern 3 across next 10 sts, P 1, work second row of pattern 2 across next 17 sts, P 1.

**Row 3 to armhole:** Work established pattern until piece measures 18″ (19″-20″) or desired length to arm-hole. End wrong side.

**Armhole:** Bind off 4 sts at the begin-ning of the next 2 rows for under-arm. Keeping first and last 3 sts in stockinette st (K on right side, P on wrong side), dec 1 st each side every other row, in the following manner:

**Row 1:** (right side) K 1, K 2 tog, work pattern to last 3 sts, sl 1, K 1, pass the sl st over the K st, K 1.
**Row 2:** P 3 sts, work pattern to last 3 sts, P 3. Continue to dec 1 st at each side every other row until 30 sts re-main. 28 (30-32) dec rows. Place re-maining 30 sts on holder to be work-ed later for neck.

**Front:** Work as for back, through armhole decreases, until 52 sts re-main. 17 (19-21) dec rows. End on wrong side. On right side, work across 17 sts, continuing to dec at armhole edge, place next 16 sts on a holder. Join a new ball of yarn and work across last 17 sts. Working with 2 balls of yarn, one for each side of neck, continue working pat-tern; dec at armhole edge every other row and at the same time, dec 1 st at each side of neck edge every other row 4 times. On last armhole dec, K 1, K 2 tog, sl the K st over the K 2 tog, break yarn and pull yarn through loop. On the other side, sl 1, K 1, pass the sl st over the K st, K 1, and on the next row, P 2 tog, break yarn and pull yarn through loop.

**Sleeve:** With No. 6 needles, cast on 40 (42-44) sts. Work in twisted rib-bing for 2″. On last row of ribbing, inc 14 (12-10) sts evenly spaced across row. 54 sts. Change to No. 10 needles and begin pattern.

**Row 1:** (right side) K 1, work first row of pattern 2 on first 4 sts, K 1, work first row of pattern 3 on next 10 sts, K 1 in back loop, work first row of pattern 5 on next 20 sts, K 1 in back loop, work first row of pat-tern 3 on next 10 sts, K 1, work first row of pattern 2 on next 4 sts, K 1.

**Row 2:** P 1, work second row of pattern 2 on first 4 sts, P 1, work sec-ond row of pattern 3 on next 10 sts, P 1 in back loop, work second row of pattern 5 on next 20 sts, P 1 in back loop, work second row of pat-tern 3 on next 10 sts, P 1, work second row of pattern 2 on next 4 sts, P 1.

**Row 3 to armhole:** Continue work-ing in established pattern, increas-ing 1 st at each side every 6th (4th-4th) row 9 (12-14) times. Work increased sts into pattern 2. 72 (78-82) sts. Work until sleeve mea-sures 17″ (18″-18½″), or desired length to underarm. End wrong side.

**Armhole:** Bind off 4 sts at the begin-ning of next 2 rows for underarm. Keeping first and last 3 sts in stock-inette st (K 1 row, P 1 row), dec 1 st each side every other row in the same manner as back decreases un-til 8 (10-10) sts remain. 28 (30-32) dec rows. Place these sts on a holder and work second sleeve.

**Finishing:** Block sweater pieces (see General Information). To assemble, sew raglan edges of sleeves to front and back. Then close side seams and sleeve seams.

**Neck ribbing:** Using the No. 6 dp needles, pick up and knit 30 back neck sts, 8 (10-10) left sleeve sts, 14 left front sts, 16 center front sts, 14 right front sts, and 8 (10-10) right sleeve sts. 90 (94-94) sts on needle. Divide sts on 3 needles. Work in twisted ribbing until ribbing mea-sures 3″. Bind off loosely in ribbing. Fold neck ribbing in half to wrong side and stitch loosely to body of sweater with yarn.

Pull all yarn ends through to the back side and weave them into the seams. Stitch down with sewing thread.

169

## Child's Pullover

### Sizes

Directions are for small size (4-6). Changes for medium (8-10) and large (12-14) are in parentheses.

| Measurements (when blocked) | Sm. | Med. | Lg. |
|---|---|---|---|
| Chest | 30″ | 32″ | 34″ |
| Length to underarm | 12″ | 13″ | 14″ |
| Sleeve length, neck to wrist | 20″ | 21″ | 22″ |
| Sweater length, shoulder to bottom | 19″ | 21″ | 22″ |

### Materials

5 (5-6) 4-oz. skeins Janknits oiled yarn or 10 (10-12) 2-oz. skeins Bernat Blarney-Spun yarn; straight knitting needles No. 6 and 10; any double-pointed needle smaller than a size 10 to use as stitch holder in making the patterns; set of double-pointed needles size 6 for neck ribbing.

### Gauge

With No. 10 needles and using the stockinette stitch (K 1 row, P 1 row), 7 sts = 2″; 5 rows = 1″.

### Helpful hints

*To increase:* Increase stitches on last row of ribbing by first knitting in the back loop of a knit stitch; then with the stitch still on the needle, knit in the front loop of the same stitch. When increasing above the ribbing on the sleeve, increase on the wrong side (this will be a knit stitch) by knitting in the back loop of the first stitch on the needle; then with the stitch still on the needle, knit in the front loop of the same stitch. On the other side of the sleeve, increase in the same manner on the last stitch on the needle.

*To join new ball of yarn:* Join yarn at edge of the piece so that yarn ends can be pulled into the seams.

*To sew pieces together:* When you finish a piece, leave about a 20″ tail of yarn for sewing together. Using a blunt needle (tapestry needle) and working from the right side, bring needle up through first stitch on the left edge. Insert needle down through center of first stitch on right edge, pass under 2 rows, pull yarn through to right side. Insert needle in center of stitch on corresponding row of left side (same place you came out on previous stitch on that side), pass under 2 rows, drawing yarn through to right side. Continue working from side to side, being careful not to pull the stitches too tight.

*To pick up neck stitches:* Use a crochet hook. Slip hook into stitches along edge, catch yarn and pull through. Transfer stitches to needle by sliding them off the end of the crochet hook onto the needle.

### Patterns

**Pattern 1:** Twisted ribbing

**Row 1:** *K 1 in back loop of st, P 1*. Repeat from * to * across row.
**Row 2:** Repeat row 1, knitting in the back loop of the K sts and purling the P sts.
Repeat these rows for pattern 1.

**Pattern 2:** Herringbone

**Row 1:** P 2, sl next 2 sts onto a dp needle and hold in back of work, K next st, then K the 2 sts from the dp needle, K 1, sl next st onto a dp needle and hold in front of work, K next 2 sts, then K st from dp needle, P 2.
**Row 2:** K 2, P 7, K 2.
Repeat these rows for pattern 2.

**Pattern 3:** Mock cable

**Row 1:** P 2, K third st on left hand needle and leave on needle, K first st on needle and slide off needle, K second st and slide off needle, slide third st off needle, P 2.
**Row 2:** K 2, P 3, K 2.
**Row 3:** P 2, K 3, P 2.
**Row 4:** Repeat row 2.
Repeat these rows for pattern 3.

**Pattern 4:** Honeycomb

**Row 1:** P 1, *sl next 2 sts onto a dp needle and hold in back of work, K next st, then K the 2 sts from the dp needle, sl next st into a dp needle and hold in front of work, K next 2 sts, then K st from dp needle*. Repeat from * to * two more times, P 1.
**Row 2:** K 1, P 18, K 1.
**Row 3:** P 1, K 18, P 1.
**Row 4:** Repeat row 2.
**Row 5:** P 1, *sl next st onto a dp needle and hold in front of work, K next 2 sts, then K st from dp needle, sl next 2 sts onto a dp needle and hold in back of work, K next st, then K the 2 sts from the dp needle*. Repeat from * to * two more times, P 1.
**Row 6:** Repeat row 2.
**Row 7:** Repeat row 3.
**Row 8:** Repeat row 2.
Repeat these rows for pattern 4.

### Directions

**Back:** With No. 6 needles, cast on 60 (64-68) sts. Work in twisted ribbing (pattern 1) for 1¾″. On last row of ribbing, inc 6 sts evenly spaced across row. 66 (70-74) sts. Change to No. 10 needles and begin pattern.

**Row 1:** (right side) P 2 (4-6), K 1 in back loop, work first row of pattern 2 on next 11 sts, K 1 in back loop, work first row of pattern 3 on next 7 sts, K 1 in back loop, work first row of pattern 4 on next 20 sts, K 1 in back loop, work first row of pattern 3 on next 7 sts, K 1 in back loop, work first row of pattern 2 on next 11 sts, K 1 in back loop, P 2 (4-6).
**Row 2:** K 2 (4-6), P 1 in back loop, work second row of pattern 2 on next 11 sts, P 1 in back loop, work second row of pattern 3 on next 7 sts, P 1 in back loop, work second row of pattern 4 on next 20 sts, P 1 in back loop, work second row of pattern 3 on next 7 sts, P 1 in back loop, work second row of pattern 2 on next 11 sts, P 1 in back loop, K 2 (4-6).
**Row 3 to armhole:** Work established pattern until piece measures 10″ (12″-14″) or desired length to armhole. End wrong side.

**Armhole:** Bind off 2 sts at the beginning of next 2 rows for underarm. Keeping first and last 3 sts in stockinette st (K 1 row, P 1 row), dec 1 st each side every other row, in the following manner:

**Row 1:** (right side) K 1, K 2 tog, work pattern to last 3 sts, sl 1, K 1, pass the sl st over the K st, K 1.
**Row 2:** P 3, work pattern to last 3

sts, P 3. Continue to dec 1 st each side every other row until 28 sts remain. 18 (19-21) dec rows. Place remaining 28 sts on a holder to be worked later for neck.

**Front:** Work as for back, through armhole decreases until 42 sts remain. End on wrong side. On right side, work across 15 sts, place next 10 sts on a holder. Join a new ball of yarn and work across last 15 sts in pattern. Working with 2 balls of yarn, one for each side, continue working pattern, decreasing 1 st each side of armhole every other row and at the same time decreasing 1 st at each neck edge every row 7 times. On last armhole decrease, K 1, K 2 tog, sl the K st over the K 2 tog and pull yarn through the loop. On the other side, sl 1, K 1, pass the sl st over the K st, K 1, and on the next row, P 2 tog and pull loop through.

**Sleeve:** With No. 6 needles, cast on 32 (34-36) sts. Work in twisted ribbing for 1¾". On last row of ribbing, inc 6 sts evenly spaced across row. 38 (40-42) sts. Change to No. 10 needles and begin pattern:

**Row 1:** (right side) P 0 (1-2), K 1 in back loop, work first row of pattern 3 on next 7 sts, K 1 in back loop, work first row of pattern 4 on next 20 sts, K 1 in back loop, work first row of pattern 3 on next 7 sts, K 1 in back loop, P 0 (1-2).

**Row 2:** K 0 (1-2), P 1 in back loop, work second row of pattern 3 on next 7 sts, P 1 in back loop, work second row of pattern 4 on next 20 sts, P 1 in back loop, work second row of pattern 3 on next 7 sts, P 1 in back loop, P 0 (1-2).

**Row 3 to armhole:** Continue working in established pattern, increasing 1 st at each side every 6th row 4 (5-6) times. 46 (50-54) sts. Work inc sts in reverse stockinette stitch with a purl row on the right side, knit row on the wrong side. Work until sleeve measures 12" (13"-15") or desired length to underarm. End wrong side.

**Armhole:** Bind off 2 sts at the beginning of next 2 rows for underarm. Keeping first and last 3 sts in stockinette st (K 1 row, P 1 row), dec 1 st

each side every other row in the same manner as back decreases until 6 (8-8) sts remain. 18 (19-21) dec rows. Place these sts on a holder and work second sleeve.

**Finishing:** Block sweater pieces (see General Information). To assemble, sew raglan edges of sleeves to front and back. Then close side seams and sleeve seams.

**Neck ribbing:** With No. 6 dp needles, pick up and knit 28 back neck sts, 6 (8-8) left sleeve sts, 10 left front sts, 10 center front sts, 10 right front sts, and 6 (8-8) right sleeve sts. 70 (74-74) sts on needle. Divide sts on 3 needles. Work in twisted ribbing until ribbing measures 3". Bind off loosely in ribbing. Fold neck ribbing in half to wrong side and stitch loosely to body of sweater with yarn.

Pull all yarn ends through to the back side and weave them into the seams. Stitch down with sewing thread.

# Woman's Wrap-around Sweater

## Sizes

Directions are for small size (36-38). Changes for medium (40-42) and large (44-46) are in parentheses.

| Measurements (when blocked) | Sm. | Med. | Lg. |
|---|---|---|---|
| Bust, including overlap | 44" | 48" | 52" |
| Length to underarm | 21" | 21" | 21" |
| Sleeve length, neck to wrist | 26" | 27" | 28" |
| Sweater length, shoulder to bottom | 30" | 31" | 32" |

## Materials

9 (9-10) 4-oz. skeins white and 1 4-oz. skein black Janknits oiled yarn or 18 (18-20) 2-oz. skeins white (natural) and 1 2-oz. skein gray Bernat Blarney-Spun yarn; circular knitting needle No. 10.

## Gauge

With No. 10 needles and using the stockinette stitch (K 1 row, P 1 row), 7 sts = 2"; 5 rows = 1".

**Helpful Hints**

*To increase:* Increase stitches on the right side by first knitting in the back loop of the stitch to be increased, then with the stitch still on the needle, knit in the front loop of the same stitch.

*To join new ball of yarn:* Join yarn at the edge of the sleeve pieces so that the yarn ends can be pulled into the seams. In working the body of the sweater, join a new ball of yarn in a place other than the front edges so the yarn ends won't show when pulled through to the wrong side.

*Two-color knitting:* With the exception of the edge stitches, this pattern is made so that it is not necessary to twist the colors as you work across the row. Simply hold one color on one finger, and the other color on another finger. This way, one color is carried below the other, and it is not necessary to twist them. For example, if you normally carry the yarn on the index finger, carry the other color on the middle finger, throwing the yarn over the left needle from whichever finger the pattern color calls for. Always carry the colors the same way; if you have the black yarn on the index finger, do so throughout the pattern so that your knitting will be as even as possible.

*To sew pieces together:* When you finish a piece, leave about a 20" tail of yarn for sewing together. Pin the right sides together and, using a blunt tapestry needle, sew pieces together using a back stitch. When joining the collar to the back of the neck, make the seam on the right side so that the fold of the collar will hide the seam.

**Directions**

**Pockets:** Knit two pieces. With No. 10 needles and white yarn, cast on 18 sts. Work in stockinette st (K 1 row, P 1 row) until 23 rows have been completed. Break off yarn, leaving a 24" tail of yarn for sewing the pocket to the sweater. Place sts on a holder to be worked later.

**Belt:** Work the belt before the sweater so that you will become familiar with the pattern. With No. 10 needles and white yarn, cast on 10 sts.

**Rows 1 and 2:** K 1, P 1 across row, ending P 1.

**Rows 3 and 4:** P 1, K 1 across row, ending K 1.

Repeat these 4 rows for pattern. Work until piece measures 60". Bind off.

**Sweater body:** With No. 10 needles and using white yarn, cast on 176 (191-206) sts.

**Row 1:** (wrong side) K 1, P 1 across the first 8 sts (front band), *K 1, P 2*, repeat from * to * across row to last 8 sts, ending K 1 (ribbing pattern), K 1 P 1 across last 8 sts (front band).

**Row 2:** K 1, P 1 across the first 8 sts (front band), *P 1, K second st on left hand needle and leave on needle, K first st on left hand needle and slide both sts off needle*, repeat from * to * across row to last 8 sts, ending P 1 (ribbing pattern), on last 8 sts, K 1, P 1 across.

**Row 3:** P 1, K 1 across first 8 sts, repeat row 1 of ribbing pattern across row to last 8 sts; on last 8 sts, P 1, K 1 across.

**Row 4:** P 1, K 1 across first 8 sts, repeat second row of ribbing pattern across row to last 8 sts, P 1, K 1 across last 8 sts. Repeat these 4 rows, working until piece measures 2½". End wrong side. K 1 row, increasing 1 (2-3) sts across the ribbing. Keep front bands in pattern as established. 177 (193-209) sts on needle, P 1 row, then begin the pattern for the sweater bottom, continuing to work front bands in white and in established pattern.

**Begin contrasting pattern:** (See following diagram.) Start at A, repeat from A to B across row, ending at C.

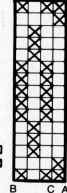

Main color (white) □
Contrasting color (black) ▣
Pattern

B    C A

When the pattern has been completed, break off contrasting color and with white, P 1 row, then K 1 row decreasing 1 st by knitting 2 sts tog after working the front band pattern on the right side of sweater. 176 (192-208) sts on needle. The pattern that has been worked on the front bands of the sweater will now be worked across the entire sweater. Work 3 rows of pattern.

**Pocket openings:** On right side, work across 25 sts, bind off next 18 sts for pocket opening, work to last 43 sts, bind off 18 sts for other pocket opening, and complete row. Continuing to work in pattern (as for front bands), work next row to pocket opening, sl 18 sts of pocket onto needle and work across these sts, work to second pocket opening and sl 18 sts of pocket onto needle and work across these sts, complete row.

Continue to work in pattern as established on front bands until piece measures 21" or desired length to underarm. End wrong side.

**Armhole:** On right side, work across first 48 (52-56) sts, bind off 4 sts for the armhole, work across next 72 (80-88) sts, bind off next 4 sts for armhole, work across remaining 48 (52-56) sts. Place front sts on a holder and work with back sts only.

**Back:**

**Row 1:** (wrong side) Join yarn and work across 72 (80-88) back sts in established pattern.

**Row 2:** K 2 tog, work in pattern across row to last 2 sts, K 2 tog. Repeat these two rows for armhole decrease until 32 (36-40) sts remain. 20 (22-24) dec rows. Bind off.

**Right Front:** Sl 48 (52-56) right front sts onto the needle and work as follows:

**Row 1:** (wrong side) Join yarn and work across row in established pattern.

**Row 2:** Work across row to last 2 sts, K 2 tog.

Repeat these two rows for armhole decrease until 28 (30-32) sts remain. 20 (22-24) dec rows. These sts will become the collar.

**Collar:** Work established pattern on 28 (30-32) sts for 0" (1"-1½"), ending at outside edge of collar. Work short rows for collar as follows:

**Row 1:** Work established pattern across first 18 sts, turn, work back across row.

**Row 2:** Repeat row 1.

**Rows 3 through 8:** Work pattern st across entire row.

Repeat these eight rows 4 times, then work two more rows of pattern st. Bind off. The collar will be wider at the outside edge because of the short rows.

**Left Front:** Work as for right front, reversing shaping. Make sure the increase rows of the collar are on the outside edge of the collar.

**Sleeve:** With No. 10 needles and white yarn, cast on 37 sts.

**Row 1:** (wrong side) *K 1, P 2*. Repeat from * to * across row, ending K 1.

**Row 2:** *P 1, K second st on left hand needle, leave on needle, K first st on left hand needle and slide both sts off needle*. Repeat from * to * across row, ending P 1.

Repeat these two rows for ribbing pattern, working until piece measures 2½". End on wrong side.

**Next row:** Knit, increasing 4 sts evenly spaced across row. 41 sts on needle.

**Next row:** Purl.

**Begin contrasting pattern:** (See diagram under Sweater body.) Start at A and repeat pattern from A to B across row, ending at C.

When the pattern is completed, break off contrasting color and with white P 1 row, K 1 row increasing 11 (15-19) sts evenly spaced across the row. 52 (56-60) sts on needle. Work until piece measures 17" (17½"-17½"), end wrong side. Bind off 2 sts at the beginning of the next 2 rows. Dec 1 st each side of every other row, in the same manner as the back decreases, until 8 sts remain. 20 (22-24) dec rows. Bind off.

**Finishing:** Block pieces (see General Information). To assemble, sew raglan edges of sleeves to back and fronts. Then close side and sleeve seams. Sew back of collar together, then stitch collar to sweater neck, easing in fullness. Stitch pockets to sweater. Weave the yarn ends into seams or back side of work, and stitch down with needle and sewing thread to secure. Try on sweater and mark location of belt loops. Crochet a chain of white yarn and attach for loops.

## Pillow

**Blocked size**
About 16″ × 16″

**Materials**

4 4-oz. skeins Janknits oiled yarn or 8 2-oz. skeins Bernat Blarney-Spun yarn; circular knitting needle No. 10; set of double-pointed needles No. 10; any double-pointed needle smaller than a size 10 to use as a stitch holder in making the patterns. For the pillow lining, ½ yard washable fabric, and washable stuffing (it takes about 12 oz. of polyester fiberfill).

**Gauge**

With No. 10 needles and using the stockinette stitch (K 1 row, P 1 row), 7 sts = 2″; 5 rows = 1″.

**Helpful hints**

Work back of pillow first so that general construction of pillow will be easier to follow. Front of pillow is constructed in the same manner, but with a pattern. Decreases are made at corners so that a square is formed. It is not possible to place markers for the decreases, but after working a few rounds the corners will be easily seen.

**Directions**

**Back:** With No. 10 circular needle, cast on 204 sts. Join work, making sure sts are not twisted.

**Round 1:** K 48, K 3 tog, K 48, K 3 tog, K 48, K 3 tog, K 48, K 3 tog.
**Round 2:** Knit.
**Round 3:** K 47, K 3 tog, K 46, K 3 tog, K 46, K 3 tog, K 46, K 3 tog. (On the dec rounds, there will be one more st before the first dec on the first side than on the other 3 sides. This is because the extra st is decreased as the 4th side is decreased.) When the round is finished there will be 46 sts between the decreases, not counting the stitch resulting from the 3 sts knit tog.
**Round 4:** Knit.
**Round 5:** K 45, K 3 tog, K 44, K 3 tog, K 44, K 3 tog, K 44, K 3 tog.
**Round 6:** Knit.
**Round 7:** Knit, dec at the corners as before. There will be 42 sts between the decreases. Continue knitting around, dec at the corners every other round. After each dec round there will be 2 sts less than the previous round between the decreases. Work on circular needle until there are too few sts to work on one needle. Change to dp needles and continue pattern until there are 12 sts remaining. Break off yarn, leaving a 20″ tail. Thread tail of yarn into a needle and pull through remaining 12 sts. Pull sts together for center and fasten off.

**Front:** With No. 10 circular needle, cast on 204 sts. Join work, making sure sts are not twisted.

**Round 1:** K 48, K 3 tog, K 48, K 3 tog, K 48, K 3 tog, K 48, K 3 tog.
**Round 2:** Knit.
**Round 3:** K 47, K 3 tog, K 46, K 3 tog, K 46, K 3 tog, K 46, K 3 tog. 46 sts between decreases.
**Round 4:** Purl.
**Round 5:** Knit and dec at corners. 44 sts between decreases.
**Round 6:** (popcorn st) K 1, *K 1, P 1, K 1, P 1, all in the next st, turn, K across these 4 sts, turn, sl 2nd, 3rd, and 4th st over first st, K 1 in remaining st, K 3*. Repeat from * to * around.
**Round 7:** Knit and dec at corners. 42 sts between decreases.
**Round 8:** Purl.
**Round 9:** Knit and dec at corners. 40 sts between decreases.
**Round 10:** Knit.
**Round 11:** Knit and dec at corners. 38 sts between decreases.
**Round 12:** Knit.
**Round 13:** Purl and dec at corners. 36 sts between decreases.
**Round 14:** Knit.
**Round 15:** Knit and dec at corners. 34 sts between decreases.
**Round 16:** (tie st) *Sl first two sts onto a dp needle and hold in back of work, wind yarn around these two sts three times, sl back onto needle and knit*. Work from * to * around.
**Round 17:** Knit and dec at corners. 32 sts between decreases.
**Round 18:** Knit.
**Round 19:** Purl and dec at corners. 30 sts between decreases.
**Round 20:** Knit.
**Round 21:** Knit and dec at corners. 28 sts between decreases.
**Round 22:** Repeat round 16 (tie st).
**Round 23:** Knit and dec at corners. 26 sts between decreases.
**Round 24:** Knit.
**Round 25:** Purl and dec at corners. 24 sts between decreases.
**Round 26:** Knit.
**Round 27:** Knit and dec at corners. 22 sts between decreases.
**Round 28:** Knit.
**Round 29:** Knit and dec at corners. 20 sts between decreases.
**Round 30:** Purl.
**Round 31:** Knit and dec at corners. 18 sts between decreases.
**Round 32:** Repeat round 6 (popcorn st).
**Round 33:** Knit and dec at corners. 16 sts between decreases.
**Round 34:** Purl.
**Round 35:** Knit and dec at corners. 14 sts between decreases.
**Round 36:** Knit.
**Round 37:** Knit and dec at corners. 12 sts between decreases.
**Round 38:** Knit.
**Round 39:** Purl and dec at corners. 10 sts between decreases.
**Round 40:** Knit.
**Round 41:** Knit and dec at corners. 8 sts between decreases.
**Round 42:** Repeat round 16 (tie st).
**Round 43:** Knit and dec at corners. 6 sts between decreases.
**Round 44:** Knit.
**Round 45:** Purl and dec at corners. 4 sts between decreases.
**Round 46:** Knit.
**Round 47:** Knit and dec at corners. 2 sts between decreases. Break off yarn, leaving a 20″ tail. Thread tail of yarn through needle and pull through remaining 12 sts, pull sts together for center and fasten off.

**Finishing:** Block pillow (see General Information). Pull all yarn ends through to wrong side and fasten down. Sew front and back together on three sides.

**Lining:** Cut fabric into two 17" squares. Join with machine stitching, right sides together and using ½" seam allowances; leave opening for stuffing. Turn to right side. Stuff pillow lining and close with hand stitches. Insert stuffed lining into pillow, and sew last side of pillow together. Pull remaining yarn ends to inside of pillow and fasten.

**Edging:** Measure out 10 lengths of yarn, 2½ yards long. Knot the yarn together at one end and attach to a chair back or door knob. Knot the other end so that it will be easier to twist, and begin twisting the yarn one way as tight as it will twist without curling. Fold the resulting cord in half and allow the cord to twist back on itself. Tie ends together so that cord won't untwist. Make three more cords in this manner. Center one cord on each side of pillow. Stitch cord along the seam with yarn, sewing through cord so stitches won't show (ends of cords will be used as tassels). At corner, wind a piece of yarn around adjoining cords, forming a tassel. Cut ends of cords free and untwist to form tassel. Trim tassels so they are even.

**To wash pillow:** (See General Information.) If the lining and stuffing are washable, the pillow can be washed without taking it apart. Blot between towels and pat into shape.

## Afghan

### Blocked size

About 60" × 44".

### Materials

19 4-oz. skeins Janknits oiled yarn or 38 2-oz. skeins Bernat Blarney-Spun yarn; circular knitting needle No. 10; double-pointed needle any size smaller than size 10 to use as a stitch holder in making the patterns.

### Gauge

With No. 10 needles and using the stockinette stitch (K 1 row, P 1 row), 7 sts = 2"; 5 rows = 1".

Note: This afghan is knit in one piece on a circular needle so that there are no seams.

### Helpful hints

*Casting on and binding off:* Leave a 12" tail of yarn and pull into fringe when finished so that the ends will not show.

*To join new ball of yarn:* Do not join a new ball of yarn at the side edges as the yarn ends will be more difficult to pull into the work neatly. Join at a place where it will not be difficult to work into the wrong side of the pattern.

### Patterns

**Pattern 1:** Wing (20 sts)

**Row 1:** K 1, P 1, K 1, P 1, sl next 3 sts onto a dp needle and hold in back of work, K next 3 sts, K 3 sts from dp needle, sl next 3 sts onto a dp needle and hold in front of work, K next 3 sts, K 3 sts from dp needle, P 1, K 1, P 1, K 1.
**Row 2:** K 1, P 1, K 1, P 3, K 2, P 4, K 2, P 3, K 1, P 1, K 1.
**Row 3:** K 1, P 1, K 1, P 1, K 2, P 2, K 4, P 2, K 2, P 1, K 1, P 1, K 1.
**Row 4:** Repeat row 2.
Repeat these rows for pattern 1.

**Pattern 2:** Popcorn-ladder (15 sts)

**Row 1:** P 1, K loosely in front loop and in the back loop of next st alternately until 8 sts have been made in the one st, draw last st tight and pass first 7 sts over it (popcorn), P 1, sl next 3 sts onto a dp needle and hold in back of work, K next st, K 3 sts from dp needle, K 1, sl next st onto a dp needle and hold in front of work, K next 3 sts, K 1 from dp needle, P 1, work popcorn st, P 1.
**Row 2:** K 1, P 1, K 1, P 9, K 1, P 1, K 1.
**Row 3:** P 1, K 1, P 1, K 9, P 1, K 1, P 1.
**Row 4:** Repeat row 2.
Repeat these rows for pattern 2.

**Pattern 3:** Double moss (24 sts)

**Row 1:** K 1, P 1 across.
**Row 2:** K 1, P 1 across.
**Row 3:** P 1, K 1 across.
**Row 4:** P 1, K 1 across.
Repeat these rows for pattern 3.

**Pattern 4:** Bramble (24 sts)

**Row 1:** (right side) Purl.
**Row 2:** *P 3 tog, (K 1, P 1, K 1) all in the next st*. Repeat from * to * across, ending with K 1, P 1, K 1 in last st.
**Row 3:** Purl.
**Row 4:** *(K 1, P 1, K 1) all in the next st, P 3 tog*. Repeat from * to * across, ending with P 3 tog.
Repeat these rows for pattern 4.

**Pattern 5:** Right-cross (2 sts)

**Row 1:** K second st on needle and leave on needle, K first st on needle and slide both sts off needle.
**Row 2:** P 2.
**Row 3:** Repeat row 1.
**Row 4:** Repeat row 2.
Repeat these rows for pattern 5.

### Directions

With No. 10 circular needle, cast on 186 sts and purl across row.

**Row 1:** Work first row of pattern 1 across first 20 sts, work first row of pattern 5 across next 2 sts, work first row of pattern 2 across next 15 sts, work first row of pattern 5 across next 2 sts, work first row of pattern 3 across next 24 sts, work first row of pattern 5 across next 2 sts, work first row of pattern 2 across next 15 sts, K 1, work first row of pattern 4 across next 24 sts, K 1, work first row of pattern 2 across next 15 sts, work first row of pattern 5 across next 2 sts, work first row of pattern 3 across next 24 sts, work first row of pattern 5 across next 2 sts, work first row of pattern 2 across next 15 sts, work first row of pattern 5 across next 2 sts, work first row of pattern 1 across next 20 sts.

**Row 2:** Work second row of pattern 1 across first 20 sts, work second row of pattern 5 across next 2 sts, work second row of pattern 2 across next 15 sts, work second row of pattern 5 across next 2 sts, work second row of pattern 3 across next 24 sts, work second row of pattern 5 across next 2 sts, work second row of pattern 2 across next 15 sts, P 1, work second row of pattern 4 across next 24 sts, P 1, work second row of pattern 2 across next 15 sts, work second row of pattern 5 across next 2 sts, work second row of pattern 3 across next 24 sts, work second row of pattern 5 across next 2 sts, work second row of pattern 2 across next 15 sts, work second row of pattern 5 across next 2 sts, work second row of pattern 1 across next 20 sts.

**Row 3:** Repeat row 1, working row 3 of all patterns.

**Row 4:** Repeat row 2, working row 4 of all patterns.

Continue working in established pattern, repeating the 4 rows of the pattern until piece measures about 60″. End the afghan on row 2 of the patterns so that the ends of the afghan will match. Bind off on right side with a knit stitch.

**Finishing:** Block afghan (see General Information). Pull all yarn ends, except ends from casting on and binding off, through to the wrong side; weave into back and stitch down with needle and sewing thread to secure.

**Fringe:** To make fringe, wind yarn around a piece of cardboard 9″ wide and cut along one end, so that each piece of yarn is about 18″ long. Use three strands of yarn for each fringe knot. To attach, fold the three strands in half to form a loop. With a crochet hook, come up through the edge stitches from the wrong side, catch the loop of yarn and pull it through to the wrong side. Pull the ends of yarn through the loop and tighten to form the fringe knot. Attach fringe on both ends of the afghan, using about three loops to every 2″. Pull the casting on and binding off ends through the loop with the fringe. After the first row of knots have been tied, tie another row about 1″ below the first row. Start at one end and tie the six strands of the first fringe knot together with the next three strands. Continue across row, tying 6 strands together—3 from one fringe knot and 3 from the next fringe knot. Combine last 9 strands for end knot (as in first knot). Lay afghan out on a table so that fringe is extended; trim so that all ends are even.

**References:**

**Stitched and stuffed art**   pages 88-91
Adapted from *Stitched and Stuffed Art*
by Carolyn Vosburg Hall, Doubleday, 1974

**Handmade toys**   pages 114-115
Adapted from *Handmade Toys and Games*
by Jean Ray Laury and Ruth Law,
Doubleday, 1975

**New uses for old laces**   pages 97-101
Adapted from *New Uses for Old Laces*
by Jean Ray Laury, Doubleday, 1974

**How to make your own "cut glass" candles**   pages 116-121
Adapted from *The Complete Book of Candlemaking*
by William E. Webster and Claire McMullen,
Doubleday, 1973